Paths to War - An Analysis of International and Regional Potential Sources of Conflict

Dr. Alwan N. Amin Eddine

BLACK HOUSE PUBLISHING

Paths to War - An Analysis
of International and Regional Potential
Sources of Conflict

Dr. Alwan N. Amin Eddine

ISBN-13: 978-1-912759-24-8

Black House Publishing Ltd
Kemp House
152 City Road
London
United Kingdom
EC1V 2NX

www.blackhousepublishing.com
Email: info@blackhousepublishing.com

BLACK
HOUSE
PUBLISHING

Contents

My special thanks to Elsa Sakis, Maya Aridi Taylor,
Professor Sarkis Abu Zeid, and
Brigadier General Elias Farhat
for the assistance they have provided in the
preparation of this book.

Introduction

We live today in the realm of Fourth-Generation warfare - warfare by Proxy in which States can manufacture and participate in war to achieve certain political and economic goals, without having their military forces directly involved.

In fact, one of the most famous expressions, "no boots on the ground" [1], used by Former US President Barack Obama during a press interview, is a clear reflection of this principle. It paved the way for manipulating existing belligerents in war zones, either to instigate confrontations with adversaries or to turn them against each other in order to weaken them.

The main purpose of this book is to identify some of today's global strategic issues, either to confirm certain existing principles, or to more thoroughly study them and highlight their different elements. It will analyze their potential impact and how to take advantage of, and/or address, them accordingly.

Hence, several geographical areas that have been subjected to huge destructive and bloody conflicts will be considered, and the so-called non-State Conflict Groups that have been exploited by States to meet their direct/indirect interests will be analyzed. Energy resources considered to be one of the key drivers of warfare will also be analyzed, as well as the strategic water canals that many States are intent on building for economic and/or political gains.

---

1   Gregory Korte. 30/10/2015. 16 times Obama said there would be no boots on the ground in Syria. *USA Today*. (Retrieved on: 25/10/2017) from: https://bit.ly/2OtC59D

Hot Spots

Balkans: The European Fergana Valley

The Balkans constitutes a real security concern for the Europeans, given their history of terrorist infiltration. It began at the end of the 20th century, especially after the war against Yugoslavia, and the dissolution of Czechoslovakia in 1992. Both of these events are deemed to have led to the end of the Soviet Union's legacy in Southern Europe.

The war against Yugoslavia was pivotal in paving the way to a new era in the region. It severed the Russian thread, specifically with the Slavic race, since it led to the division of Yugoslavia which was considered a remnant of the Soviet era.

Consequently, Russia was prevented from being able to re-establish its presence in the Southern and South Eastern regions of Europe. On the other hand, the European Community and the United States also recognized the independence of separate Balkan territories such as Croatia (which joined the EU on 1/7/2013, and NATO on 1/4/2009), Slovenia (which joined the EU on 1/5/2004, and NATO on 29/3/2007), Bosnia & Herzegovina (which joined in 1992), and Montenegro (which joined the NATO on 5/6/2017) making all the necessary arrangements leading them to join the EU and the North Atlantic Alliance - further expanding NATO's influence in the Region to the detriment of Russia.

This scenario led the French military expert General Didier Tauzin to say: "the Balkans will soon become a base for Jihadists and an incubator for terrorist attacks against Europe. Therefore, Europe and its policies will come under pressure, and this will trigger large scale warfare in Europe, the Middle East and Africa. The return of the Jihadists will engender huge problems for the

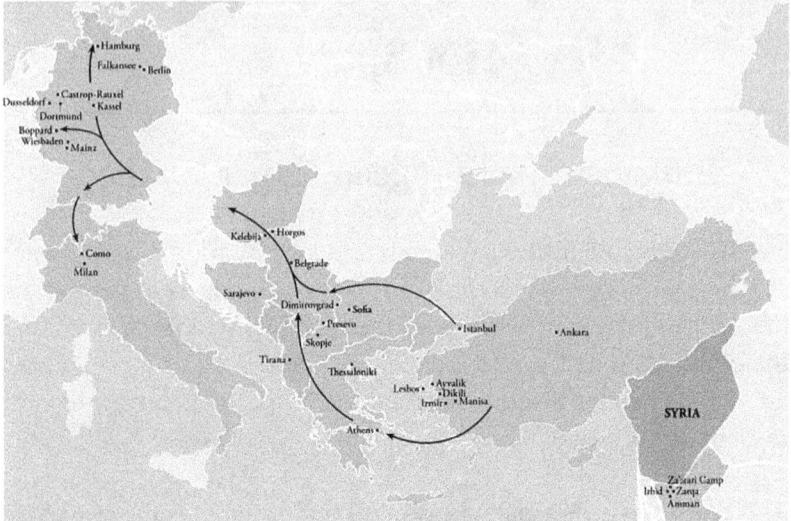

Part of immigration routes to Europe likely to be taken by terrorists
residing in the Levant

Europeans, particularly the French. Our future will be dark and uncertain in the coming years."[1]

Georgetown University Terrorism researcher and expert Bruce Hoffmann said: "Though many ISIS fighters were killed, thousands survived and managed to flee from Syria. Some of them are certainly hiding in the Balkans where they keep a low profile and wait for an opportunity to sneak into Europe."[2]

Dr. Vedran Dzihic, Senior Researcher at the Austrian Institute for International Affairs, indicated that "Salafist, Jihadi and Islamist extremists are in the Balkans and their infrastructure is intact, and they are now focused on certain countries and on the region as a whole."[3]

1   Samar Radwan. 27/12/2017. General Tauzin: The Balkans, a new terrorism "incubator"... Europe faces a "dark" future. Sita Institute. (Retrieved on: 12/1/2018) from: https://sitainstitute.com/?p=1274

2   In the aftermath of the ISIS fall in Syria and Iraq: the fighters where to? 12/2/2018. Al-Azhar Observatory for Combating Extremism. (Retrieved on: 24/2/2018) from: https://bit.ly/2t2GF98

3   Boris Georgievski. 1/6/2017. Could Balkan nations become the new hotbeds of

Preparing the Ground

Data indicates that since the 1990s the Arab and Turkish roles have greatly influenced the Bosnians. Following the participation of the so-called Jihadists in the Bosnian war, several Arab countries, namely Gulf Cooperation Council (GCC) States, began financing "the construction of many mosques and Islamic educational institutions. Arab and Turkish students and tourists started pouring into Bosnia & Herzegovina. Bosnian Cities became the monuments of Arab countries' largest investments and commercial centers."[4]

This led to the emergence of extremism within the Balkan community. In fact, the assistance provided by some Islamic governments was to gain political influence rather than humanitarian aid. Extremism in the region rose simultaneously with the arrival of those donations, like many political and religious leaders who said: "everyone knows that the region is infested with cells promoting extremism, and that many members were arrested. It is unanimously agreed that political Islam is not currently a threat to the country and that it is still under control. However, it will soon become a huge danger and a big challenge for the community and the state in the future." At the end of the Yugoslavian war, NATO forces began entering the Balkans, especially war-torn Kosovo, providing humanitarian assistance to their citizens following the destruction of homes and facilities, and infrastructure. In addition, many NGOs also were intervened, some of them "gave rise to the most dangerous threat in post-war Kosovo: Religious extremism." In fact, Kosovo started complaining about organizations that "were only aiding the Muslim population, even though the vast majority of the Balkan residents, 95% of whom were Albanians, saw

---

Islamist Extremism? DW. (Retrieved on: 3/5/2018) from: https://bit.ly/2GWX9BZ

4   Abdul Rahman Ammar & Mamish Nadad. 18/5/2016. Is salafism threatening moderated Islam in Bosnia and Herzegovina? DW. (Retrieved on: 6/3/2018) from: https://bit.ly/2HUpMRx

themselves as one people fighting for one cause, that is, the end of Serbian oppression. So why were foreign aid organizations discriminating against people based on religion?"[5]

Meanwhile, according to reports, the Albanian authorities, partnered with the CIA to uncover a terrorist network operated by the former Al-Qaeda leader Osama Bin Laden, who was accused of masterminding the American Embassy bombings in both Nairobi and Dar es Salaam of August 1998. The network's objective was to use the Albanian Muslim territory as an epicenter for terrorist operations in Europe, in addition to the serious threat of enabling Osama Bin Laden to personally visit Albania.[6]

On May 17th, 2017, during a parliamentary session held in Berlin, the German government acknowledged another problem that had the potential to accelerate: The fall of the Balkans to extremism due to the influence of powerful GCC states, especially in Kosovo, where their "influence has grown more dramatically in the last decade, due to the difficult socio-economic conditions in the region and the general lack of opportunities, especially for youth."[7]

Throughout these successive events, many observers consider that Bosnia & Herzegovina has one of Europe's largest numbers of combat fighters under ISIS as compared to the country's population. Most of the alleged Jihadists come from remote villages under Salafist control. Over the course of the last two decades, traditional Bosnian Islam entered into competition with parallel Salafist entities, which recently triggered a reaction from

---

5   Amjad Malaeb. 22/11/2014. Will Kosovo be the gate of European Political Islam? Al-Akhbar Lebanese Newspaper. Issue No.: 2451. (Retrieved on: 10/2/2018) from: https://bit.ly/2FGF37K

6   Bin Laden opens European terror base in Albania. 29/11/1998. American Council for Kosovo.(Retrieved on: 10/3/2018) from: https://bit.ly/2FIosmm

7   Boris Georgievski. Could Balkan nations become the new hotbeds of Islamist Extremism? Op. cit. from: https://bit.ly/2GWX9BZ

the moderate Muslim community, but many see this reaction as being too late."[8]

Training Centers

Prior to the breakup of the former Yugoslavia, radical Islamists came from the Middle East and other parts of the world to fight for the cause, where they fought as volunteers with Bosnian Muslims. After the war, some of them married local women and became residents. With the outbreak of the Arab Spring, the flow of fighters started to flow in the other direction.[9]

Initially, these groups established military training centers for limited sessions in areas like Oryahovitsa and Jelznopole in Zenica and Zawiercie under the guise of setting up Youth Camps. Here, young people were systematically transferred to national parks, local hills, forests and other secure locations to be trained under the supervision of former Mujahideen. As a result, this area has witnessed a growth in radical Islam encouraged by the West.[10]

As for ISIS, the organization has at least "five military training camps in Kosovo, located in remote areas near the self-proclaimed republic's border with Albania and Macedonia citing a source close to the intelligence services. According to the source, the largest camps are situated in areas adjacent to the towns on the Urosevac and Djakovica line as well as the Decani District, while the smaller camps are located in the Prizren and Pec regions." So, the youth are "brainwashed there and they also learn Arabic and study the Koran, something that is followed by so-called combat practice training, headed by former members of the Kosovo

8   Abdul Rahman Ammar & Mamish Nadad. Is salafism threatening moderated Islam in Bosnia and Herzegovina? Op. cit. from: https://bit.ly/2HUpMRx

9   Kosovo and the Balkans: A Fertile Ground for Islamic Terrorism. June 2017. Investigation Journalism. Issue No.: 65. (Retrieved on 10/3/2018) from: https://bit.ly/2GdEse5

10   Andishe Sazan. 28/7/2016. The role of Wahhabism in recruiting the youth into terrorist groups. Arabi Press. (Retrieved on: 8/6/2017) from: https://bit.ly/2CRBKHE

Liberation Army (KLA)." In this regard, the director of the Center for Balkan Studies in Pristina, Fadil Lepaja, noted that "Kosovo's borders with Albania and Macedonia exist only on paper that makes tracking of Islamists' training camps almost impossible."[11]

Some reports indicate that over 350 Bosnians joined ISIS, making it the seventh country in the world in terms of contribution. Kosovo provided a similar number of combatants to Abu Bakr al-Baghdadi, making it the largest. Other countries in the area also sent Jihadists to Syria and Iraq: 150 in Syria and 200 in Iraq from Albania, and 100 and 150 respectively from Macedonia, while Montenegro and Serbia only contributed a handful of combatants. Rumors spread that the UCK, or the Kosovo Liberation Army (KLA), fought the war of independence against Serbia and set up a number of training camps for Jihadists before being officially dismantled. However, it still benefits from widespread local public support, and since the conflict with Serbia took a religious twist, the UCK is now closer to Islamic extremism.[12]

Additionally, several observers claim that the US and EU leaders have provided little vital intelligence to Bosnia & Herzegovina in its fight against terrorism, which aims to halt the growing Jihadist activity on its territory. In fact, Bosnian Muslims, known as Bosniaks, provide the largest number of ISIS fighters per capita, permitting seasoned foreign fighters to rest, change identities, obtain weaponry, gain easy access to laundered money and surreptitiously enter Western European nations. More than 60 of the 200 Jihadists groups called Jamaats operate in Bosnia alone.[13]

---

11   Kosovo's ISIS Camps – Creche for Young Terrorists. 23/7/2016. South Front. (Retrieved on: 10/3/2018) from: https://bit.ly/2oZclaX

12   Kosovo and the Balkans: A Fertile Ground for Islamic Terrorism. Op. cit. from: https://bit.ly/2GdEse5

13   Richard Pollock. 14/6/2017. West Ignores Growing Terrorist Threat from ISIS Bosnian "Safe Havens". The Daily Caller. (Retrieved on: 10/3/2018) from: https://bit.ly/2rjZ7Vn

The Classification of the Jamaats

Information from the German government states that the Balkan terrorists "do not only join ISIS, the former Al-Nusra Front, but approximately 10% of Islamist fighters are fighting with different factions of the Free Syrian Army (FSA). The number of people traveling to Syria and Iraq from Bosnian villages, dominated by Salafi thinking, is increasing significantly. These are villages where people's religious and social lives are governed by ancient Islamic customs and traditions."[14]

Furthermore, observers also point to another organization known as The Grey Wolves, an extremist Turkish movement operating under the umbrella of the Turkish Intelligence Services. Within its ranks are former Turkish intelligence officers or retired military contractors. Its primary objective, the establishment of a single state stretching from the Balkans to Central Asia, is inspired by the history of the Ottoman Empire, which brought under its authority many states in Asia, Europe and Africa.[15]

Lack of Information or Intentional Negligence?

Western intelligence organizations, specifically in Europe, retrieve limited security information about serious threats to Europe and other parts of the world, however the question that is always asked is: Is there a huge lack of information because these Jamaats and organizations have the ability to conceal information and their plans, or are intelligence services intentionally refraining from collecting such data and information?

For example, the German government does not rule out the "potential threat imposed by insurgent radical Islamic

---

14 Nemanja Rujević. 25/1/2018. Is the Balkans a breeding ground for terrorism? DW. (Retrieved on: 29/3/2018) from: https://bit.ly/2HX0sdo

15 Grey Wolves. 24/2/2018. Al-Yawm Channel. (Retrieved on: 23/4/2018) from: https://bit.ly/2F4fJLV

individuals and enclaves in Bosnia & Herzegovina, and there is communication between radical Islamists from the Balkans and Germany. However, the German intelligence service is unable to access tangible information about growing Islamic ambitions in Bosnia." The German government also states that data on the numbers of terrorists coming from Bosnia & Herzegovina and Kosovo who joined Jihadist groups over the last few years need special attention. Media reports state that these two Balkan countries (i.e. Bosnia & Herzegovina and Kosovo) export the highest number of Islamist extremists per capita from Europe.[16]

In this regard, Christian Democratic MP, Gregor Golland, demanded security inspections of all refugees living in North Rhine-Westphalia. As MP and CDU security affairs expert, he criticized a former statement by the Minister of Interior, Ralf Jäger, who said, "No terrorists came from the Balkans to Germany". Golland considered this statement naïve, adding, "to date, we are not even able to confirm the identities of all the refugees."[17]

In addition, a German press report stated that the Federal Intelligence Service (BND) was participating in a covert operation headed by the United Sates to counter potential terrorist threats by ISIS fighters coming from Syria and Iraq. On February 3rd 2018, the German magazine *Der Spiegel* reported that the BND was part of operation Gallant Phoenix, which had been ongoing since October 2017 in collaboration with 21 other countries.[18]

The Federal prosecution said that German police arrested a terrorist cell planning to carry out explosive belt attacks on

16   Nemanja Rujević. Is the Balkans a breeding ground for terrorism? Op. cit. from: https://bit.ly/2HX0sdo

17   Terrorist cells infiltrate to Germany via the Balkans. 2/6/2016. European Center for Counterterrorism and Intelligence Studies. (Retrieved on: 27/5/2018) from: https://bit.ly/2FHOwf6

18   Jassem Ramahi. 26/2/2018. The Lords of Fanaticism in Europe. (Retrieved on: 7/6/2018) from: https://bit.ly/2FH6Pkq

the main street of Heinrich-Heine-Straßein central Düsseldorf. Spiegel Online said that the discovery of the cell was further proof ISIS had put Germany on its target list. According to the Rheinische Post, police chief Norbert Fiesler told the newspaper "we have been directly involved in investigations from the start", adding that the police had updated their information based on the results of the investigations and that security measures for the city center had been strengthened.[19]

The British *Daily Telegraph* published a report stating that in an attempt to prevent radicalization, a number of British universities have asked kitchen staff and janitors to spy on their students. Many universities opted for this action as they believed that students may feel more comfortable expressing radical tendencies in restaurants, cafeterias, or libraries rather than in lecture halls. The *Telegraph* also published details of training programs that university staff undertake to spy on students.[20]

In France, on the other hand, General Didier Tauzin believes that the French government will not prosecute ISIS returnees coming from Syria, namely because "France lacks the means to do this. France's view of world politics is different from that of the people, especially the French. Nonetheless, the truth remains that French Jihadists are traitors supporting the enemy against the French and the world, and should be prosecuted."[21] Some observers believe that the majority of European Intelligence services have not yet adopted a consistent policy to deal with domestic extremism and terrorism. In terms of Europe specifically, The European Commission has not yet imposed any standard security policies or common guiding principles in the fight against terrorism or extremism within its territory.

---

19   Terrorist cells infiltrate to Germany via the Balkans. Op. cit. from: https://bit.ly/2FHOwf6

20   Jassem Ramahi. The Lords of Fanaticism in Europe. Op. cit. from: https://bit.ly/2FH6Pkq

21   Samar Radwan. General Tauzin: The Balkans, a new terrorism "incubator"... Europe faces a "dark" future. Sita Institute. from: https://sitainstitute.com/?p=1274

According to reports, Europe tops the list of radical Islamism with 1,300 extremist organizations operating within its border, which have been able to operate unaffected for years within plain sight of European intelligence.[22]

Subsequently, the Director of the Department for New Challenges and Threats in Russia's Department of Foreign Affairs, Ilya Rogachev, confirmed that many terrorists fleeing Syria and Iraq are trying to return to their homelands via Turkey and Ukraine. He believes that the Western states brought this problem on themselves, saying: "We have always warned against the politicization of security cooperation; however, the West encouraged Ukraine to move forward with anti-Russianism. The European Union granted Ukrainian citizens the right to cross into the West without a visa, making it possible for armed returnees to infiltrate the European Union through its borders." Rogachev also affirmed that the issue with the terrorists is not their access to the Middle East, it is that thousands of them leaving the area to be dispatched all over the world. He stressed that most of them do not return to their home country as they know security authorities will be waiting for them. Therefore, other states will suffer the consequences for the Returnees.[23]

Serious Concerns

According to a report issued in January 2018 by Conflict Armament Research, one-third of ISIS weaponry, which consists of automatic rifles and rocket launchers, were sourced in the European Union, namely Romania, Hungary, and Bulgaria. Thousands of foreign fighters have also fled the conflict zones. A large number of them remain in the Balkans[24] waiting for the

---

22   Jassem Ramahi. The Lords of Fanaticism in Europe. Op. cit. from: https://bit.ly/2FH6Pkq

23   Ukraine becomes a bridge for armed groups into Europe. 31/3/2018. Russia Today. (Retrieved on: 15/7/2018) from: https://bit.ly/2GHwlJx

24   Abdullah Mustafa. 7/10/2018. European cooperation with "Balkans" in the issue of returned fighters from conflict zones. Asharq Al-Awsat. Issues No.: 14558. (Retrieved on: 7/10/2018) from: https://bit.ly/2C1UmIn

appropriate moment to infiltrate the rest of Europe.[25] Meanwhile, a French official source says that out of 1,700 French fighters heading to Syria and Iraq since 2013, 400 to 450 were killed, and about 250 returned to the French territories.[26]

Balkans expert, Henry Jones, says no one knows what is happening in the areas where they live. They have their own security forces and the police are not usually allowed to enter, neither are those who are not a part of their groups.[27]

Gordon N. Bardos, president of SEERECON a strategic advisory and political risk-analysis firm for clients doing business in southeast Europe, affirms that these Jamaats have "established these radical-controlled villages that almost function as extraterritorial enclaves within Bosnia. They set up these enclaves in remote villages in the region, establishing financial networks to transfer money, providing people with new identities or false identities." Bardos continues "We are talking about people involved in the 9/11 bombings. We are talking about guys involved in the USS Cole attack. We are talking about guys who were involved in the U.S. Embassies in Africa back in August of 1998. All these guys were operating in the Balkans in the 1990s. And they kind of sowed the seeds for a lot of what we are seeing now."[28] The arrest of Kosovar Jihadists who were preparing for a terrorist attack in Venice, Italy, in March 2017 shows how close the region is tied to the real threat. Khalid Massoud, the man who attacked Westminster in London, claimed to be a radicalized Kosovar citizen.[29]

---

25 Jassem Ramahi. The Lords of Fanaticism in Europe. Op. cit. from: https://bit.ly/2FH6Pkq

26 In the aftermath of the ISIS fall in Syria and Iraq: the fighters where to? Op. cit. from: https://bit.ly/2t2GF98

27 Richard Pollock. West Ignores Growing Terrorist Threat From ISIS Bosnian "Safe Havens". Op. cit. from: https://bit.ly/2rjZ7Vn

28 Ibid.

29 Kosovo and the Balkans: A Fertile Ground for Islamic Terrorism. Op. cit. from: https://bit.ly/2GdEse5

An Aimless Future

"Political Islam receives support from non-governmental sources in the Middle East," said the deputy foreign minister of Kosovo, Petrit Selimi, who believes that this danger poses a challenge to the democratic political process. Selimi said the threat would be a major obstacle to Kosovo's bid to join the European Union, where his country had a stake in the participation of some Jihadists fighting with Takfiri groups in Syria and Iraq. This was a fact confirmed by the President of the Republic Advisor Garentina Kraja.[30]

"There is no doubt that the recruitment process is possible thanks to a network of Salafist places of worship," says Assad Hasmovich, a Bosnian journalist specializing in terrorist groups. "The establishment of a caliphate or Islamic homeland is the main motivation for these young jihadists, especially with the growth of foreign fighters participating in the Balkan conflicts over the years, in addition to the presence of fighters from the Balkans participating in multiple conflicts around the world which only add to the problem."[31]

Jasmin Ahic, assistant professor and terrorism specialist at the University of Sarajevo's Criminology Department, warned against "the threat coming from the returnees not only for having fought in the belligerent countries, but also for never coming back the same after such experiences." He added: "They are certainly under the surveillance of security authorities. However, the danger lies in their tendency to recruit other candidates to the conflict."[32]

On the other hand, the Balkans expert Vedran Dzihic does not

---

30   Amjad Malaeb. Will Kosovo be the gate of European Political Islam? Op. cit. from: https://bit.ly/2FGF37K

31   Bosnia, a fertile ground for Jihadist elements in the Middle East. 20/4/2015. Al-Arab Magazine. (Retrieved on: 6/3/2018) from: https://bit.ly/2oz6jO5

32   Ibid.

think the situation in the Balkans is a major threat but warns that risk indicators should be taken seriously. "It is clear that there is a phenomenon that will keep pace with the development of the Balkan countries in the coming years and decades, but it is also clear that the Western Balkans will not return to what it was before the 1990s," he said, adding that any increase in extremism would be dependent on development in the region, "if security problems, instability and economic difficulties continue to increase, extremism will increase."[33]

Similarly, according to some experts, the security threats associated with Kosovo are linked to both the return home of radical fighters from the Middle East and the impact of Jihadist propaganda on a largely disenfranchised and unemployed local youth.[34]

Understandings and Objectives

Based on the above, several conclusions can be made:

- It seems that one of the goals behind the creation of this new situation is to halt Russian expansion into the European continent. This is reminiscent of the objective which drove regime change in Iran in 1979, when Imam Ayatollah Khomeini came to power declaring that his policy principles were neither Eastern nor Western. The same applies to the crisis in Afghanistan which was created to prevent the former Soviet Union from accessing oil sources in the Arabian Peninsula and diminishing its threat on US national security. Similarly, the CIA established Al-Qaeda in the 1980s due to National Security Adviser, Zbigniew Brzezinski's instructions.

- Threatening Europe with terrorism serves to keep it under

---

33   Boris Georgievski. Could Balkan nations become the new hotbeds of Islamist Extremism? Op. cit. from: https://bit.ly/2GWX9BZ

34   Kosovo and the Balkans: A Fertile Ground for Islamic Terrorism. Op. cit. from: https://bit.ly/2GdEse5

NATO's umbrella since it gives them a reason to pressure the Europeans into taking a stance on important issues. However, the biggest problem is the ability to keep Lone Wolves under control as they are able to get off leash and strike the Old Continent at its core.

- The purpose may also be to turn these Jamaats into artificial barriers on the coast of the Mediterranean in order to keep at bay any future European expansion, specifically towards Africa. This would also harm the Russian interests in Mediterranean and African oil and gas.

- The gap between the Muslim Arab world and the Christian West serves to benefit the conflicts and interests of some of the major sates, namely the United States which has a relatively ideal geopolitical position in the world. In addition, these situations also benefit Transcontinental Multinational Corporations as well as weapons and oil Cartels.

- Terrorism is used as a direct or indirect pretext to infiltrate countries and instigate regime change as in the case of the Arab Spring, or to establish military bases for further influence. For instance, under the pretext of combating terrorism, Western military bases, namely American, were established in the northern part of Syria under the pretext of fighting terrorism, even though the operations of terrorist organizations, in Syria particularly, are coming to an end. It should be noted that the Official Syrian News Agency, SANA, quoted local sources as saying that the International Coalition transferred terrorist groups[35] on military patrols from Al-Sadd camp in the southern countryside to an unknown destination. Military helicopters used in the process took off from the suburbs of Sadd Al-Basel in south Al-Hasakah. According to the same sources, this was

---

35   Dr. Bashar al-Jaafari, Syria's permanent representative to the United Nations, stated that some transferred terrorists from Syria were arrested along the Algerian – Niger borders asking who sent them there. For more details, see: "Al-Mashhadiya" program with Dr. Bashar al-Jaafari. 1/3/2019. Al Mayadeen. (Retrieved on: 6/3/2019) from: https://bit.ly/2H3sbMq

the same organization previously transferred by the Coalition from eastern Deir ez-Zor, more precisely from Al-Shuitat villages. The Russian Coordination Center, in Hmeimim, confirmed that the Washington-led International Coalition continues to cooperate with the remnants of terrorists in Syria. It stressed that US military trainers are establishing new military units under the name of The New Syrian Army near a refugee camp in the city of Al-Hasakah, from groups splintering from terrorists.[36] It is reminiscent of what happened after the dismantling of Yugoslavia where many observers believe that the goal of the US war in the Balkans specifically aimed to "establish US key military bases in the so-called military Triangle of the Albanian - Balkans region, through the establishment of the Camp Bond base in Kosovo (in addition to the Ramstein Air Base in Germany which is the headquarters of the American Armed Forces in Europe, and the AFRICOM headquarters) which provides logistics services to the Balkans, the Mediterranean, Central Asia, and the Middle and the Near East."[37]

The German Geo-Political Role in the Middle East

The German influence is expanding in many areas across the world, both politically and militarily as a peacekeeper. There is little doubt that Germany is considered to have one of the strongest economies in the world and was able to resist the 2008 world economic crisis and contain its repercussions, becoming the key driver and most prominent player in the European Union. In addition, Berlin is accepted and welcomed as the face of Europe especially to the Middle East countries.

---

36   SANA: American helicopters transfers an ISIS group to an unknown direction. 31/12/2017. Russia Today. (Retrieved on: 7/8/2018) from: https://bit.ly/2lqeU49

37   Samar Radwan. 27/2/2018. Balkan Wars directed against "continental" Russia. Luke Michel (3/3). Sita Institute. (Retrieved on: 23/9/2018) from: https://bit.ly/2CQTX8m

Militarily, several observers consider that Germany dared break one of its greatest barriers imposed on it after the end of WWII, by creating a Command Center for its forces operating abroad. This Command Center is important since it could easily be converted into a center of command for its entire military force, both internal and external, and in addition it could assist in rebuilding military command cadres. This was preceded by the 1994 controversial ruling, by the German Constitutional Court, that allowed for German military involvement in operations abroad, provided this was done within the framework of international organizations such as the United Nations or the NATO, and assuming approval by the Parliament.[38] This ruling violated the provisions of the German Constitution that clearly limited the function of the army to within the borders of the country.

Subsequently, some analysts believe that Germany started implementing this policy, especially on the European level, following Russia's annexation of the Crimean Peninsula in 2014. This act was, in Berlin's opinion, a breach of international laws and regulations and a sign of another Russian expansion in the Continent. It raised many concerns despite good relations between the two countries in the past.

With regard to the Middle East in recent history, Germany was and still is interested in the Asian countries bordering Europe, especially those in the Arab Levant. Consequently, Germany became closer to the Ottoman Empire and suggested the building of a railway linking Berlin to Bagdad and Mosul through Istanbul, in an attempt to access the warm water and India.[39]

On the other hand, some believe that this project was an Ottoman initiative rather than German. It was proposed by the Ottoman

---

38   Abdu Mubashar. 22/6/2001. The German Army at the beginning of a New Century. Al-Ahram Egyptian Newspaper. Year: 125. Issue No.: 41836. (Retrieved on: 17/5/2014) from: https://bit.ly/2It5HVA

39   Abdel Karim Hassan Khodeir. 2006. The Bagdad-Berlin Express franchise. linking the east to the west. Al-Jarida Iraq. (Retrieved on: 8/6/2018) from: https://bit.ly/2I6JngU

Sultan, in agreement with Germany, for two reasons: firstly, Germany's policies did not allow for expansionist plans, and secondly, the Sultanate was at the brink of collapse and wanted to catch-up with Europe.[40]

Regardless of the two points of view, Germany would have benefitted from this railway, which, if implemented, would have been a lifeline for Germany to the Levant and from there further to the East.

Some scholars point to a recent German interest in the Middle East, the so-called European Initiative, which reflects the European Union's opinion on the situation in the region and how to change and reform it. This initiative was the focus of a meeting between former US President George W. Bush, and former German Chancellor Gerhard Schröder during his visit to Washington in March 2004 in which a joint European-American initiative was launched for the Middle East. "However, the US out maneuvered Europe and launched another Greater Middle East initiative."[41] This has led many researchers to say that the Middle East is witnessing the re-establishment of a new German policy, which lies in the quest for the East in a broad sense "from Asia to the Middle East to Africa."[42]

Presence in the Mediterranean

Germany sought to have a foothold on the Mediterranean Sea, exploiting Greece's economic crisis in 2010 in an attempt to force it to sell uninhabited islands. Consequently, the former Greek Prime Minister George Papandreou stressed that Greece did not need to sell any of its uninhabited islands for money to cover its

---

40   Marc von Lüpke - Schwarz / Shams Al-Iary. 23/5/2013. The true story of the Levant Express. DW. (Retrieved on: 3/5/2018) from: https://bit.ly/2qiEoEp

41   Rana A. Al-Rifai - Dr. Mohamad Qubaisi. 2004. The United States and the new Middle East. Dar Al-Haref Al-Arabi Publishing. Beirut – Lebanon. First Edition. P: 153.

42   Mohamed Nohman Jalal. 3/6/2010. The East-oriented German politics: Lessons for the Arab world. Al-Wasat Bahrain Newspaper. (Retrieved on: 19/3/2018) from: https://bit.ly/2FXF45T

budget deficit. "I think there are more creative solutions to the deficit than the sale of Greek islands," Papandreou told reporters after meeting German Chancellor, Angela Merkel, in Berlin.[43]

German MPs called on Greece to sell its islands to pay off its debts. The broad-based *Build* newspaper summed up the idea by saying: "We give you cash, you give us Corfu." Liberal MP Frank Schafler told the paper "The Greek state should refrain from entering into joint-stock companies, but rather should sell real estate like the uninhabited islands". However, MP Marco Wanderwitz from Chancellor, Angela Merkel's party, said: "If the European Union, hence Germany agreed to provide financial assistance to Greece, the latter has in turn to agree on some guarantees" adding "a few islands are enough".

Figures from the Greek Ministry of Tourism state that the majority of its six thousand islands are uninhabited. According to *Build* newspaper, a private company based in Hamburg sought to sell an uninhabited Greek island for 45 million EUR. In 1993, controversy arose between Germany and Spain when German members of Parliament suggested buying the island of Mallorca, a major German tourist destination.[44]

On a military level, sources indicate there has been a German desire to be present in the Middle East since the time of former German Chancellor Gerhard Schröder. This was practically achieved under Chancellor Merkel, within the framework of NATO or the UN. Effectively, this presence has become seemingly normal,[45] especially after the adoption of the Security Council Resolution 1701 that was issued in the aftermath of the 2006 Israeli war

43 Alwan N. Amin Eddine. 2017. Sino - German Relations 1990 – 2015: In Light of Economic Strategies and Policies. Isticharia. Beirut – Lebanon. First Edition. P: 455.

44 Greece will never sell "Islands" to face financial crisis. 7/3/2010. Al-Eqtisadiah. (Retrieved on: 6/4/2018) from: https://bit.ly/2rvMJCZ

45 Salah Nayouf. 5/6/2014. An analysis of the German Policy for the Middle East's fundamentals and variables. Al-Moatamar Iraqi Newspaper. (Retrieved on: 28/5/2018) from: https://bit.ly/2rBg3s7

on Lebanon, when the German navy began its presence in the Eastern Mediterranean off Lebanese territorial waters.

In the same context, Germany has played a prominent role in the mediations that took place in prisoner exchange negotiations between Israel and other parties such as Palestinian Hamas and Lebanese Hezbollah. Not only did it play this important role, but over time it also became a pivotal, though silent, regional actor. Germany is perfectly able to balance its relations with Israel and with neighboring countries, contrary to what many see as a US obvious bias in favor of Israel, which triggers a lot of sensitivities from the people and governments of the region.

Furthermore, Germany also marks its presence through arms deals, a topic that will be tackled later on. The most noteworthy of these deals is the mutual deal between German and Israel in which Germany sold Dolphin-class nuclear submarines to Israel. Under former Chancellor Helmut Kohl and during the first Gulf War, Israel was promised this type of submarine.

In 2000, Kohl lost his office and the government of former Chancellor Gerhard Schröder handed over the first batch of submarines to the Israel navy. The mission was accomplished at that time by German former Foreign Minister Yushka Fisher himself. On the last day of Schröder's mandate, the Chancellor signed a deal which allowed for Israel to be supplied with two more submarines of the same type. Israel now possesses five submarines and is set to acquire two additional ones in the near future.[46]

On October 23rd 2010, Israel also signed a deal with Germany to purchase three submarines, a step considered to be strategically important by Israeli Prime Minister, Benjamin Netanyahu, who said the memorandum of understanding is of "strategic

---

46 Germany sells submarines to Israel... and Iran reaps the profits! 13/1/2017. Al-Raya Qatari Newspaper.(Retrieved on: 15/1/2018) from: https://bit.ly/2K7gXUM

importance for the security of Israel. Signing it reflects the commitment of Germany and Chancellor, Angela Merkel, to the security of Israel and the close cooperation between both countries."[47]

In Syria, on the other hand, several field sources reported the arrival of a German military unit on the outskirts of the city of Manbij, whose objective was to support the Syrian forces with ground troops in their battle against the terrorist organization ISIS. The unit linked and coordinated military operations between the Coalition's air force and the troops on the ground, it also had several other tasks including incursions, street fights, and de-mining missions.[48] However, the German Ministry of Defense denied any presence of German military forces in northern Syria. The Ministry spokesman claimed these accusations were untrue, saying that "no German Special Forces operate in Syria".[49] Yet Germany's approval to dispatch military forces in Syria in support of French troops, following the assaults they encountered on November 13th, 2015, implies the contrary.

Information gathered indicated that Berlin decided to dispatch approximately 1200 soldiers in military aircrafts and warships to fight the terrorist group, ISIS, in what is considered one of Germany's most important foreign missions[50]. The German minister of defense, Ursula von der Leyen, said that her government had to make tough decisions that were important and necessary, while Chancellor Merkel promised Germany's support during talks with former French president, François

---

47   Germany agrees to sell three submarines to Israel. 24/10/2017. Al-Jazeera. (Retrieved on: 21/12/2017) from: https://bit.ly/2KQ6iia

48   The arrival of German military forces to Syria. 14/6/2016. Sputnik. (Retrieved on: 7/2/2018) from: https://bit.ly/2K3dlDd

49   Damascus condemns German and French military presence in Syria, and Berlin denies it all. 15/6/2016. Al-Mayadeen. (Retrieved on: 19/6/2017) from: https://bit.ly/2wwYbUC

50   Germany about to dispatch 1200 soldiers in support to France to fight ISIS. 30/11/2015. Assafir Lebanese Newspaper. (Retrieved on: 25/3/2016) from: https://bit.ly/2rv2kDX

Hollande, pending her parliament's approval.[51] However, a worrying report published by the German newspaper, Build, referred to the arrival of armed forces in northern Syria, including German fighters in support of Olive Branch operation, spearheaded by Turkish forces. In fact, the International Freedom Battalion was formed of soldiers from different nationalities, including Germans. This was confirmed by leaked video footage that confirmed the presence of German soldiers amongst the elements of the Battalion.[52]

Presence in the Levant

Following multiple disagreements between Berlin and Ankara, the German Cabinet approved the withdrawal of its forces based in the Turkish Incirlik Air Base, adopting instead the Minister of Defense Ursula von der Leyen's plan to relocate forces to the Al-Azraq Airbase in Jordan rather than to the NATO one in Turkish Konya.[53] Being based in Jordan gave Germany military presence in the heart of the Middle East rather than on the sidelines in Turkey.

German activity in Iraq is considered significant, especially on the Kurdish side, where it sold additional weapons to local military forces after ISIS took control of large parts of Iraq and Syria in 2001, under the pretext of offering training and help. In this context, on February 16th, 2018, the German Minister of Defense was particularly keen to support the Peshmerga forces after a joint meeting, saying: "The meeting was excellent, in

---

51   Germany joins the military campaign against ISIS upon a request from France. 26/11/2015. Reuters. Prepared by: Sameh Al-Bardissi. (Retrieved on: 17/9/2018) from: https://bit.ly/2jJs23d

52   Mustafa Al-Buhairy. 28/1/2018. Are German forces fighting against Turkey in northern Syria? Arabi 21. (Retrieved on: 19/5/2018) from: https://bit.ly/2nnA1Ef

53   Germany withdraws its forces from Turkish Incirlik to Jordan. 7/6/2017. Al-Alam News. (Retrieved on: 8/7/2018) from: https://bit.ly/2I2LNBq
Also see: Nathalia Abdallah. 22/6/2017. Germany moves its military from Turkey to Jordan. Russia Today. (Retrieved on: 17/9/2018) from: https://bit.ly/2KKeX5M

fact, we are pleased with the mutual trust that has emerged over the last few years and the excellent relations between the two parties (Germany and Kurdistan)."[54]

It is worth noting what Germany's former Foreign Minister, Sigmar Gabriel, said during his visit to the Kurdish-controlled region of northern Iraq: "The defense of the Peshmerga and their fight against the organization of the Islamic state at the same time defends the security of Germany."[55] This clearly demonstrates the close relations between the two parties and explains the concentration of about 150 German soldiers near Erbil to train Kurdish forces.[56]

With regard to the sale of weapons to the Kurds, a growing number of German parliamentarians expressed their support for Germany's export of arms to the Peshmerga forces under the condition that German allies and the Kurdistan Regional Government request such support. "Normally, I am against the export of German arms, but since Germany is an important source of weapons, in this particular case, the export of arms becomes legitimate if other countries cannot do so" said Gregor Gizi, head of the parliamentary bloc on the German left.

Frank Walter Steinmeier, Foreign Minister, prior to taking office as German President, noted that in principle, his country was ready to concede on its policies firmly prohibiting weapon exportation and provide the Kurdish fighters with the necessary weapons in their fight against ISIS in northern Iraq.[57]

---

54 German minister of defense: keen to support the Peshmerga. 16/2/2018. Rudaw Media Network. (Retrieved on: 7/7/2018) from: https://bit.ly/2Hhi035

55 German foreign minister: the German security is being protected in Iraq. 20/4/2017. DW. (Retrieved on: 6/9/2018) from: https://bit.ly/2G6ly8Y

56 From the Kurdish to the Iraqis, a shift in the German support. 12/2/2018. Enab Baladi. (Retrieved on: 6/8/2018) from: https://bit.ly/2HekVJI

57 Charlotte Beck. 28/8/2014 Germany's New Foreign Policy in the Making: Initial Reactions to the Iraq Crisis in Review. Heinrich Böll Foundation. Arabized by: Ola Saleh. Edited by: Hayed Hayed. (Retrieved on: 16/3/2018)

During a conversation with a subject matter specialist, the expert claimed that Masoud Barzani, the Kurdish leader, required all those who wanted to supply him with weapons be from Germany. This claim is supported by Germany's submission of some 20,000 rifles and 1,000 anti-tank missiles to Peshmerga forces. However, relations between the two parties became colder when Germany did not recognize the referendum on the independence of the Kurdistan region from Iraq. The German position was in favor Kurdistan remaining within the Iraqi territories. Professor Ferhan Sedar from the Mustafa Barzani Section for Kurdish Studies at the Erfurt University in Germany said that "there was a belief that Germany would take a reserved position since many Kurds live here in Germany and the country is also significantly involved in arming the Kurds."[58]

According to a paper on German military presence in the region, Berlin clearly desires balanced relations with both the Kurds and Bagdad. This paper was to be deliberated by the government on March 6th, 2018 before submission to the Parliament. It outlines how a "balance between the Iraqi central government and the Kurdistan region of Iraq"[59] could be achieved.

Regarding the training of the armed forces, the German Defense Minister pointed out that the new mission of the German soldiers would be "to support the Iraqi Government security forces in Baghdad in their battle against the remnants of the 'State' (i.e. ISIS) operating in Iraq." She explained that the German army would support the Iraqi security forces in the field of health and logistics upon a request from the Iraqi government. She also stressed the importance of continuing the partnership with Iraq in the long term, noting that her country sought to stabilize and

from: https://bit.ly/2HemfMx

58 Matthias von Hein. 26/9/2017. Kurdistan's referendum – Concerns in Berlin and disappointments in Erbil. DW. (Retrieved on: 8/3/2018) from: https://bit.ly/2FyfxDT

59 Aref Jabo. 5/3/2018. A new mission for the German military... an upcoming mediation between Bagdad and Erbil. DW. (Retrieved on: 7/8/2018) from: https://bit.ly/2oWpm4t

maintain the victories achieved[60], especially after the German government decided to expand its military mission in Iraq and other areas[61] to include the training of government forces to fight terrorism, assisting in the demining process, and to increase the number of German military 'advisors' in Iraq from 140 to 800.[62]

This came after the agreement between the German Ministries of Defense and Foreign Affairs to build the capabilities of the Iraqi army by sending soldiers specialized in the education and training of trainers. The German Minister of Defense said: "All my interlocutors insist on their continued desire for Germany's participation (in support of) Iraq,"[63] which means a major change and expansion of the functions of German forces in the region, which had been limited to participation in reconnaissance operations.[64]

This position is consistent with that stated by former Foreign Minister, Sigmar Gabriel that the withdrawal of German troops from Iraq would send the wrong signal and would increase the risk of a new civil war. As a matter of fact, he previously urged the German parliament or Bundestag to extend their military mission to train the Peshmerga Kurdish forces in Iraq. He said: "The more international organizations increase their activities in the region, the lower the risk of a new escalation. Our withdrawal will convey the wrong message to the parties in the conflict, as if we accept the threat of a new civil war"[65], adding

---

60   From the Kurdish to the Iraqis, a shift in the German support. Op. cit. from: https://bit.ly/2HekVJI

61   Germany: Extending six foreign military missions with 2600 soldiers involved. 7/3/2018. Site 24. (Retrieved on: 16/3/2018) from: https://bit.ly/2oVmhld

62   The German government decides to expand its military mission in Iraq. 7/3/2018. Elnashra. (Retrieved on: 8/7/2018) from: https://bit.ly/2Fkm85Q

63   Aref Jabo. A new mission for the German military... an upcoming mediation between Bagdad and Erbil. Op. cit. from: https://bit.ly/2oWpm4t

64   Ibid.

65   Gabriel warns against withdrawing German forces operating in Iraq, and

that their involvement would be limited in training armed forces. "Of course, we will not go there with security officers... Some people might see the permanent presence of foreign security forces as foreign occupation of their country."[66]

On the other hand, a group of German soldiers, known as Darmstädter Signal, were critical of the situation of their army and warned against the planned expansion of the German military mission in Iraq. The group's spokesman, Florian Kling, said: "No, they cannot do this. We do not even have airplanes to relocate troops on the mission, the situation with regard to providing human cadres and equipment is turbulent and will bring the German army to the verge of collapse." He added that the German military mission in Iraq would become riskier in the future when the training of al-Baghdadi soldiers to fight terrorism begins, bearing in mind the initial German mission was only limited to train Kurdish fighters in Northern Iraq. He warned against "the risk of falling into explosive booby traps. This whole thing may end badly...the chaos in Iraq was instigated by the Americans and they must bear responsibility for it. We have many other responsibilities, like the ones in Mali and Afghanistan, which I see as more useful."[67]

Despite the opposition it faces at home, Germany's position on increasing its military duties in Iraq, whether training or logistics, is an indication of Berlin's desire to intervene in some international crises, especially as the guidelines for arms exports stipulate that no export approvals be granted to countries involved in armed conflicts, places suspected of being involved in future conflicts, and/or if these exports could potentially prolong tensions.[68]

---

urges the Bundestag to extend its mission. 8/11/2007. Al-Sumaria. (Retrieved on: 13/6/2017) from: https://bit.ly/2FkwlPs

66 German foreign minister: the German security is being protected in Iraq. Op. cit. from: https://bit.ly/2G6ly8Y

67 German Soldiers: the German army on the brink of collapse. 7/3/2018. Asharq al-Awsat Newspaper. (Retrieved on: 11/7/2018) from: https://bit.ly/2I6ZGuu

68 Charlotte Beck. Germany's New Foreign Policy in the Making. Op. cit. from:

Iran: the Gate to Central Asia

Iran is one of the most coveted states in the region, especially following the lifting of economic sanctions in mid-January 2016, based on the signing of a nuclear agreement. Some writers point to Germany's role in laying the foundation stone for the Iranian nuclear issue in 1974, when the Consortium of German Power companies, a subsidiary of Siemens, under the rule of Shah Mohammad Reza Pahlavi, signed an agreement to build the first nuclear reactor in the area of Bushehr. The works at the reactor were suspended after the outbreak of the revolution and the return of Ayatollah Khomeini to power, under whom the governing system switched from a pro-Western regime to one hostile against the old system and policies. Being a member in the Bagdad Pact, the United States was one of the countries to race for nuclear cooperation with Iran in 1959, supplying it with the first technical nuclear research facility, and in 1967 contributed to the establishment of the first nuclear research center in Tehran in cooperation with the Atomic Energy Organization of Iran (AEOI).[69]

In a remarkable position, following US President Donald Trump's decision to withdraw Washington from the nuclear negotiations[70], the German Foreign Minister, Heiko Maas, announced that his country would remain committed to the nuclear deal, pointing out this served political interests. "Our purpose is clear", Maas told journalists. "We remain in the nuclear deal to serve our political and security interests, and we will make sure this deal will have a certain future."[71]

On an economic level, many researchers believe that Iranians

---

https://bit.ly/2HemfMx

69   Nabil Sabib. 23/5/2006. Germany and the Iranian nuclear file. Al-Jazeera. (Retrieved on: 17/2/2017) from: https://bit.ly/2oN7R9w

70   Trump withdraws from Iranian nuclear agreement. 9/5/2018. Al-Hayat Newspaper. (Retrieved on: 2/9/2018) from: https://bit.ly/2K9fvRR

71   German foreign minister: Berlin will remain committed to the Iranian nuclear deal as it serves political interests. 9/5/2018. Al-Manar. (Retrieved on: 14/5/2018) from: https://bit.ly/2K6TRO9

have a fondness of Germans, stemming not only from the quality of German products, but also from their economic values. "It does not have to include any cultural missions," said German businessman Frank Michael Rosh. "It is very arrogant to export your cultural concepts alongside your products. This is why Iranians, who are always anxious about Western cultural agendas, are attracted to Germany."[72] The German government also strongly invested in cultural exchange and personal diplomacy, a successful approach by Berlin, making it one of the few players in the region with both a good reputation and influence. It gives grants and assistance, in addition to educational exchange programs and other topics. Moreover, Germany is considered to be Tehran's first European, asserting that it is the bridge between Europe to Iran.[73]

During his February 3rd visit to Iran in 2016, Frank Walter Steinmeier said that 10 prominent German economic and political delegations visited the Islamic Republic of Iran in 2015 and deliberated with its Iranian partners. He noted that 8 other prominent economic delegations were waiting to visit Iran to pave the way for common investment opportunities.[74] In a fierce race to access the Iranian market, the German multinational Siemens signed agreements on railway infrastructure. A spokesman for the company said that once the sanctions were lifted, the multinational would enter into negotiations with the Iranian state to improve the railway infrastructure sector.[75] This sector in Iran is one of the most important and sought after, in which China and other countries compete, in the global market, to build rail networks and fast trains.

---

72 What are German businessmen doing in Iran? 3/11/2015. Noon Post. (Retrieved on: 27/3/2017) from: https://bit.ly/2qtapGb

73 Lauren Harrison, Germany, the silent player in the Middle East. 16/11/2014. Noon Post. (Retrieved on: 3/6/2017) from: https://bit.ly/2jHvBGX

74 Germany tightens it relations with Iran. 3/2/2016. International Institute for Iranian Studies. (Retrieved on: 29/6/2017) from: https://bit.ly/2rvyfUG

75 Siemens anticipates a lift of sanctions and signs a railway deal with Tehran. 8/1/2016. Al-Arabiya. (Retrieved on: 17/4/2017) from: https://bit.ly/2qmAqaU

Germany, after Italy and China, is one of Iran's main trading partners. Berlin is trying to return to this market strongly, especially after the sharp drop in the level of trade between the two countries since 2005.[76]

As for the Central Asia Gate, the German government extended its military mission in Afghanistan and increased the size of those forces[77], which is the third largest international force in this war-torn country, allowing 980 soldiers to participate in the NATO mission, up from the previous number of 850. Germany allowed its army to be present in the region without taking part in hostilities.[78] Germany returned and renewed its presence there because of the dire security situation that led to the decision.[79]

In Uzbekistan, Germany occupied the Termez military base located at the borders with Afghanistan, making it the only country allowed to conduct military operations with this state. In turn, Germany contributed to the development of the city's infrastructure.[80] However, it declared the shutdown of this military base after a 14-year presence in the city.[81]

In conclusion, André Wüstner, president of the German Armed Forces Association, stressed the need to increase the number of German soldiers, noting that when the reforms were introduced in 2001, under which the army size was reduced, no one expected

---

76   Paul Belkin. 20/5/2009. German Foreign and Security Policy: Trends and Transatlantic Implications. Congressional Research Service. P: 22.

77   Yassin Buteity. 7/10/2017. Germany considers increasing its troops in Afghanistan. Russia Today. (Retrieved on: 18/3/2018) from: https://bit.ly/2HUjuj

78   Germany extends its forces' mission in Afghanistan until the end of 2016. 1/11/2015. France 24. (Retrieved on: 15/11/2017) from: https://bit.ly/2oVGjtQ

79   Germany: Extending six foreign military missions with 2600 soldiers involved. Op. cit. from: https://bit.ly/2oVmhld

80   German soldiers will be able to stay in Uzbekistan. 12/12/2005. Elaph. (Retrieved on: 16/10/2017) from: https://bit.ly/2ruAKqk

81   Germany Formally Closes Uzbekistan Air Base. 17/12/2015. Silk Road Reporters. (Retrieved on: 12/1/2016) from: https://bit.ly/2FZkXEc)

a crisis to arise, including the Ukrainian crisis and the war on terrorism, making this action necessary.

The year 2016 witnessed the mobilization of over 20 thousand soldiers.[82] In addition, the German Minister of Defense revealed a plan to increase the number of fighter tanks and armored personnel carriers, and to equip the army's heavy weapons systems. The Minister seeks to invest 130 billion Euros in military armament over the following 15 years.[83]

---

82   An increase in the German forces mission due to escalation of international tasks, 5/12/2015. European Center for Counterterrorism and Intelligence Studies. (Retrieved on: 18/11/ 2017) from: https://bit.ly/2wpgk6R

83   German minister of defense plans for an increase in the army's tank numbers. 27/1/2016. Afri-gate News. (Retrieved on: 18/10/2017) from: https://bit.ly/2pva7zg

Syria Unified… A Russian Imperative

There is no doubt that Russia played a very important role in the radical transformation of the New World Order. On October 4th, 2011, the Russian Federation used its veto power in the Syrian crisis for the first time, announcing the beginning of a new phase in international relations. This event was not necessarily aimed at resolving the Syrian issue as much as it was to show a practical end to the uni-polar system that had reigned the world since the 1990s. Russia's position on the Syrian issue had to do with reviving the principle of balance of power in international relations, away from hegemony and dictatorial policies.[84]

Hence, Syria occupies a prominent position in the new Russian Vision, especially since many researchers in international relations believe that the war on Syria is the basis for the restructuring of the New World Order.

A unified Syria is imperative since any division of it, including the so-called safe or useful Syria, will negatively impact Russia's reconstruction efforts and its desire to revive the Westphalia Principles in international relations. The main principles of the Westphalia are centered in the full respect for the sovereignty of States, and non-interference in their internal affairs, the violation of which will never be willfully accepted by Russia.

Russia's Eurasian Project

With regards to Russia's Eurasian Project, the following should be clarified:

---

84   Alwan N. Amin Eddine. 18/6/2017. The Strategic Dimension of the Russian Involvement in the Syrian Crisis. Baissour - Aley, in the framework of a dialogue symposium held by the *Syrian* Social *Nationalist Party west coordination department with the Russian ambassador to Lebanon Dr.* Alexander Zasypkin: To follow the news, see: Zasypkin in Baissour: the west seeks to sustain its expansionary policy whereas Russia strives to end hegemony. 19/6/2017. NNA. (Retrieved on: 15/3/2048) from: http://nna-leb. gov.lb/ar/show-news/290369/

- Firstly, if Russia were to accept the dismantlement of a state, it may be self-destructive since Russia itself is composed of several republics, multiple ethnic, racial, and religious groups. These elements originate in regions neighboring the Russian Federation, including Turkey, the Caucasus, and central Asia, which are a source of danger to Russia. Other states, such as Turkey and Iran, will not be spared from the negative impact of state division.

- Russia's adoption of the Eurasian Theory, which was initiated on the ground with the creation of the Eurasian Federation, requires the existing administration in Moscow to maintain a united Syria, especially as it forms an essential part of the Rim Land that protects the Heartland. Any cracks or fissures affecting this Rim Land will rebound on Russia itself. In addition, the Levant region is considered the meeting point that joins the three continental circles of Europe, Asia, and Africa. Syria is the heart of the Levant, since, historically, it has been the knot that has connected transportation corridors for thousands of years. Caravans coming from the Levant would cross the Palmyra oasis before heading south towards the Arabian Peninsula, north towards Anatolia and Rome, or west towards Egypt and North Africa.

- Syria is the last Mediterranean coastline accessible to Russia, and losing it has a deep impact. Therefore, in order to keep it, Russia signed a new agreement with the Syrian government guaranteeing Russian presence in the port of Tartus to ensure its survival in the future. Russia has also started building a new base in the town of Khirbat Ra's al Wa`r near Bīr al Qaşab district east of Damascus. This will be Russia's third permanent and declared presence on Syrian territory (after the port Tartus and Hmeimim). The planned location of the Russian base is 50-km from Damascus, 85-km from the disengagement line in the Golan, and 110-km away from the southern Golan hills. It is also 96-km from Jordan and 185-km away from Al-Tanf military base near Iraq.[85] Moreover, Russia is also trying to expand its influence in the Mediterranean by seeking to attract other countries to their project, such as Turkey and Egypt, and to establish new military bases, as in Cyprus for example.

- The concept of a Safe Syria was only a first step in the endeavor to free remote areas. The goal of Russian airstrikes was not only to secure useful areas, but also the strategic areas outside of the useful equation, such as Deir ez-Zor. Safe Syria was only a prelude to keeping critical areas under control while leaving the periphery for timely action at a later stage. The biggest example of this was the advance of Syrian Armed Forces into the desert in an attempt to reach borders with Iraq. They reached the periphery of Ar-Raqqa district, heading south to secure border with Jordan. Once settled there, the Syrian Army declared that the As-Suwayda district territories were terrorist-free, and that the corridors being used to transport armed groups and their ammunitions coming from the south towards Ar-Raqqa were closed.[86]

- The de-escalation zones, in terms of their clauses, were not made for bargaining purposes. Rather, politically speaking, they mark a circumvention of concepts which were previously not satisfactory for adversaries. In this sense, new different concepts were generated while maintaining a cease-fire or a cessation of hostilities component. This is from a political perspective. However, on a military level, these zones are a way to create a buffer between fighters and focus on more dangerous areas in the field. It also gives the Syrian Forces and their allies the opportunity to settle, and then move military forces to more critical areas where the Syrian Army needs further reinforcement once the de-escalation understanding is ratified.

---

85   The reason behind Moscow building a military base in the Syrian desert. 17/7/2017. Elmarada. (Retrieved on: 14/3/2018) from: https://bit.ly/2vsUThg

86   The Syrian Army fully controls As-Suwayda desert. 9/8/2017. Al-Mayadeen. (Retrieved on: 15/9/2017) from: https://bit.ly/2vtMlqs

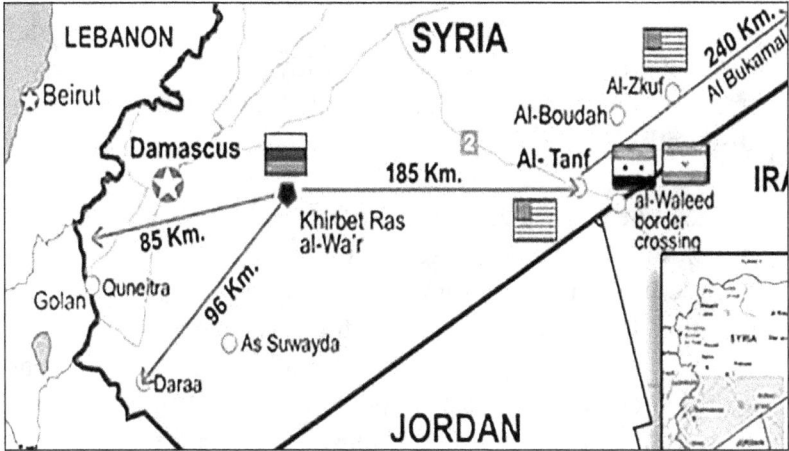

The Third Russian base in East Damascus

- Russia will not start its Eurasian Project with failure, especially since it has many hopes. Its failure in Syria could lead to many concerns among some of the countries that are members of the project or candidate states.

- If Russia accepts the division of Syria it would mean a loss of its hard-won gains. Strategically speaking, this would be a huge mistake especially after the major transformation it has induced in the region. The Syrian crisis has had major repercussions not only on the region, but also internationally. It clearly exposed the cracks and fissures in the World Order that followed the 1992 collapse of the Soviet Union, which, along with other setbacks, laid the foundations for a New World Order, the face of which is still to be determined.

The Syrian Reality

The current situation in Syria is as follows:

- The Russian Foreign Minister, Sergey Lavrov, was clear about the issue of the safe areas. He threw the ball on the Syrian court by linking Russia's approval of this solution with the consent of Syria itself, which the Syrian government is unlikely to accept. In addition, Russia will likely be harder to deceive in Syria, as it was in Libya, and will not easily approve the creation of safe zones that may be the prelude to dismantling the country.

- Some writers argue that Russia's idea of federalism in Syria is merely an attempt to appease the opposition parties in particular, in order to find a compromise formula that avoids the idea of partition. In fact, it conducted meetings with many of the parties involved and made serious efforts to hold common gatherings aimed at ending the crisis. These efforts came simultaneously with reconciliations that ended tensions over hotspots.

Regional Partners

The issue of Syria has political ramifications that not only impact Syria internally but also the surrounding countries.

- The division of Syria will certainly lead to the establishment of sectarian and ethnic cantons which would negatively affect Russian relations with Iran and Turkey, especially if the Kurds seized the opportunity to establish their own sphere of influence. This would have several repercussions on both countries. To avoid this, the Turkish forces engaged in the Olive Branch Operation in Afrin despite Turkey's (opposing) stance on the Syrian issue as a whole. As a matter of fact, Turkey only needed a pretext to intervene and create a de-escalation zone on its southern borders. It feared that Syria's division, as well as the creation of Kurdish cantons, could be the prelude to the dismantlement of Turkey itself.

- Safe zones in Syria further tickles Turkey's fancy by changing positions on its agreements with Russia with regards to maintaining Syria's unity and territorial integrity. Therefore, many analysts believe that Turkey's involvement in Syria was one of the repercussions of the meeting between the Russian and Turkish presidents in Ankara on October 2016, when the Syrian crisis topped the meeting. In fact, the Turkish involvement that aimed at creating buffer zones was a requirement suggested since the beginning of the Syrian crisis but nothing had been done about this up until that point. So why did it happen only after the meeting? Most probably, Russia tolerating Turkey's intervention was a way of involving the latter in its war on terrorism, therefore putting pressure on it to stop the infiltration of terrorist groups through its territory.

The Essence: International Rules and Regulations.

The Russian position, according to official statements, does not go beyond the application of the rules and provisions of international law, the most prominent being:

- During the many conferences held to resolve the Syrian crisis, Russia's position was always clear since it always demanded the preservation of Syrian unity. Recently, Turkey, Iran, and the decisions of the Astana and Sochi meetings have highlighted the need for full adherence to the principle of the territorial integrity of Syria.

- Russia is a proponent of the implementation of the rules and decisions of the Westphalia conference, the most important of which is to ensure respect for the integrity and sovereignty of states. This is clearly an attempt to halt American endeavors, designed by the Neo-Conservative parties, the most important of which are preemptive and preventive wars, in addition to forcibly induced regime changes.

- Russia refuses to accept the resignation of the Syrian president before his mandate expires since he symbolizes the country's unity. Russia's reluctance to violate international law is founded on its belief that it could set an international precedent and the international community may use this as leverage against Russia in the future. Although it is true that there is room for interests to lead to common action and land division, sharing the Syrian geography would constitute an immense threat and therefore Russia's only solution is Syria's unity.

Hence, the foreign military presence in Syria makes Russia accepting Syria's division very suspicious. In fact, the two countries have a secret Sykes-Picot like agreement or at least understandings around certain areas of influence. In this regard, it is important to mention the following:

- According to reliable sources, the so-called Kerry - Lavrov agreement was published by the Russian Foreign Ministry in Russian on its website, and was clear and transparent in its position since the agreement did not include any items expressing a desire to share Syrian lands.

- It is true that Russia and many Kurdish leaders share good relations, and that Russia insisted on inserting the Kurdish issue in the Geneva Negotiations, however, this was more of an attempt to pressure Turkey into closing the corridors through which fighters were infiltrating Syria, rather than an endeavor to create an independent state or entity outside the legitimate government of Syria.

- Practically speaking, the Kurdish area cannot be a prelude to land division especially since the region is full of Syrian, Russian, American and Turkish armed forces, notwithstanding other foreign-supported armies such as the Syrian Democratic Forces. Hence, they form a sort of barrier that prevents Kurdish areas from joining forces. Furthermore, there are considerable disparities within the Kurds themselves regarding their region and its future.

- Some political analysts believe that indicators "confirm the existence of a Turkish-American agreement which states that the US gives Turkish forces complete discretion to launch a ferocious war against the PKK (Kurdish Workers' Party) and its branch in Syria, namely the Kurdish People's Protection Unit, in return for Turkey and its army's diligent participation in the war against the Islamic State and its agreement to establish no-fly zones in the northwestern part of the Syrian territory at a depth of approximately 50 miles and a length of 100 miles." Analysts added that the United States sold its Kurdish allies to entice Turkey to wage war against the Islamic State[87], as this would serve its future interests.

• The ratification of a new constitution based on Federalism in Syria does not mean partition but rather a solution which guarantees the rights of minorities, namely the Kurds, and puts an end to Western attempts to intervene in the Syrian crisis on the pretext of defending these minorities and ethnicities. Russia and the United States are both federal countries, not to mention that the Iraqi constitution has adopted federalism in its texts.

• Russia considers any foreign military presence in Syria not within the understandings of the legitimate Syrian government to be an occupation, according to the rules of international law, and should be resisted by all means. This is a clear sign that no understandings exist outside the general framework of matters.

All in all, a unified Syria is quintessential for Russia in every respect.

---

87   Abdel Bari Atwan. 11/8/2017. "Has America forsaken its Allies for safe zones in Syria and for Turkey's involvement in an internecine war against the "Islamic State"? When is this regional war taking place? What will be the outcome? Rai Al-Youm. (Retrieved on: 12/12/2017) from: http://www.raialyoum.com/?p=299483

Striking Pakistan... Compelling Reasons

The American President Donald Trump has made some striking statements on the role of Pakistan in fighting terrorism. According to some international news reports, Pakistan must "end the deceitful game it is playing. It is not entitled to receive money for fighting terrorism while conducting secret operations with those who are seeking to destroy Afghanistan."[88] Consequently, the pace of escalations in Washington - Islamabad relations increased considerably. The former Pakistani Foreign Minister, Khawaja Muhammad Asif, attacked the United States during a meeting with representatives of Pakistani parliamentary political parties to discuss the latest recent tensions between Pakistan and the United States. Asif said: "the patience that our country has shown must not be interpreted as a weakness". He pointed out that the US position towards his country is only an attempt to "make Pakistan responsible for the US failures in Afghanistan since the invasion (2001)."[89]

After Washington announced the suspension of its financial aid to the Pakistani army, amounting to approximately 255 million dollars a year, the Pakistani army stated that the Commander of its armed forces told a senior US military commander that "the entire Pakistani nation felt betrayed by recent statements issued by the Americans, given their decades of cooperation."[90]

Geo-Strategic Positions

Pakistan holds an important position on the Asian Rim. For example, the Pakistani coast on the Pacific is more than 1000 km long, and it is the country that encloses Afghanistan, as well as Iran, blocking their access to Pacific waters.

---

88   Times: Pakistan must end its lies and deceit. 6/1/2018. Rai Al-Youm. (Retrieved on: 17/2/2018) from: https://bit.ly/2mm8D9v

89   Pakistan strikes Trump with fiery statements in reaction to his accusation of terrorism: "Do not think that our patience towards you is a sign of weakness!!" 6/1/2018. Horria Post. (Retrieved on: 19/3/2018) from: https://bit.ly/2D6RaNi

90   Pakistan Commander in Chief: We felt betrayed upon US criticism. 12/1/2018. Reuters. (Retrieved on: 18/2/2019) from: https://bit.ly/2D7Sq1Q

Given this, Washington needs Islamabad to access, or remove, its combat units fighting in Kabul, because the alternative, using Iranian territory (whether by land, sea or air), would be difficult, if not impossible. Not to mention its new military cooperation with China – a topic that will be addressed later. In addition, Pakistan largely oversees the Strait of Hormuz and the Arabian - Persian Gulf, where oil convoys come and go to the world from that region.

In addition, Russia seeks to embrace Pakistan following the differences between Islamabad and Washington, as it works to strengthen military, diplomatic and economic relations with it, which could turn historic alliances in the region upside down in a stark transformation from the situation in the 1980s when Pakistan assisted the US in smuggling weapons and spies across the border to support Afghan fighters in their fight against the Soviets.[91] Khurram Dastgir Khan, Pakistan's Defense Minister said: "It is an opening... Both countries have to work through the past to open the door to the future."[92]

Gas Lines

Pakistan is vital to current and future gas pipeline transit routes to India and China. This is something Washington dreads, since most of the countries with large energy reserves are located in a region which is, politically speaking, not Washington-friendly. Therefore, Washington couldn't keep the pressure more on

---

91 Quoting official sources, the Pakistani Express Tribune said that the US military transferred the leader of ISIS terrorist organization Abu Baker Baghdadi there. It confirmed that a prominent Iranian official told a delegation under the chairmanship of the Attorney-General for Pakistan (A.G.), Ashtar Ausaf Ali, that Iran holds reliable intelligence reports stating that the US relocated "ISIS" elements and leader Abu Baker Baghdadi to Afghanistan. For more details, see: Baghdadi hiding... Iran reveals a US plan to reiterate the Iraqi scenario in two states. 28/5/2018. Sputnik. (Retrieved on: 26/8/2018) from: https://bit.ly/2sccny6)

92 Drazen Jorgic. 6/3/2018. With gas and diplomacy, Russia embraces Cold War foe Pakistan. Reuters. (Retrieved on: 13/9/2018) from: https://ara.reuters.com/article/worldNews/idARAKCN1GI1ME

Beijing in the future and the siege it wants to impose on China, will be broken progressively; especially since the US wants to prevent Beijing's access to energy by closing its land and sea trade lines in order to stop its economic expansion which hits at the heart of Washington.

The TAPI Line

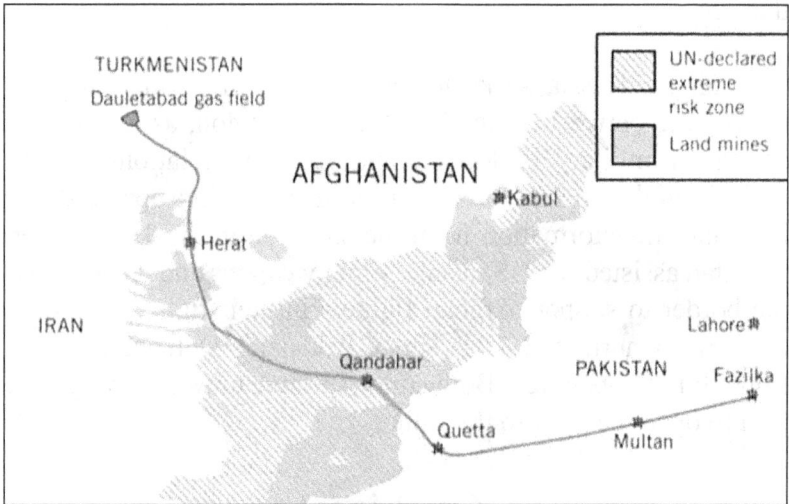

TAPI Gas Pipeline

The TAPI line is the 1814 km long gas pipeline which links Turkmenistan to Afghanistan and India through Pakistan, a project which began in 2015. The Turkmen President, Gurbanguly Berdimuhamedow, declared that the parties are working on the construction of the TAPI Gas pipeline on the Afghan territories. Berdimuhamedow also stated that "Turkmenistan is currently building this pipeline on its lands. Contributors are also working together to solve technical issues related to its continued construction on the Afghan lands."[93]

---

93   Turkmen President: Works are ongoing for the TAPI pipeline project in Afghanistan. 3/7/2017. Youm 7. (Retrieved on: 18/1/2018) from: https://bit.ly/2qZhiE7

The Iran - Pakistan Line

Due to the security risks still surrounding Afghanistan, Pakistan is able to build an alternative pipeline coming from Iran[94], which is estimated to have the third largest gas reserve after Russia and Qatar. Data suggests that Iran, which completed the installation of 900 km of pipeline, threatened to fine Pakistan 200 million dollars due to the slow completion of the project.[95]

Subsequently, the Russian company Gazprom signed a memorandum of understanding with Iran's National Oil Company to cooperate on the development of gas fields in Iran and its transfer to India through Pakistan. According to a statement issued by the Russian company: "The two companies can start preparing an economic and technical study for the design, build and operation of the Iran-Pakistan-India gas pipeline."[96]

China's Thirst For Energy

This project will be a tributary and a protector of the 30-year-old Siberian gas pipeline, which will be pumped in the year 2021, at a cost of $ 400 billion. Therefore, there will be no more fears for the future of Chinese industry and production, especially as it will reduce environmental pollution produced by Chinese production as per the world's request of Beijing. The first Silk Road Investment Fund project was announced in Pakistan on April 20th 2015 during the visit of the Chinese President. According to the joint statement issued by the two countries, the fund will inject capital in the Asian Investment Company of the Three Gorges Company of China to develop a hydropower project in Pakistan in addition to other clean energy projects.[97]

94   Pakistan and Iran discussions to activate gas transportation projects. 2/6/2018. Al-Alam News. (Retrieved on: 5/7/2018) from: https://bit.ly/2sAqrAz

95   Will Iran avail from fining Pakistan for a gas pipeline? 13/5/2014. Al-Alam News. (Retrieved on: 28/7/2017) from: https://bit.ly/2D65K7Z

96   Moscow and Tehran agree on the construction of the Iran-India gas pipeline. 3/11/2017. Russia Today. (Retrieved on: 8/6/2018) from: https://bit.ly/2h2QnzK

97   The Silk Road fund starts its first investments in Pakistan. 21/4/2015. Arabic.

Pakistan and Russia may sign a multibillion-dollar contract to buy gas from Moscow. In addition, Russia has appointed an honorary council in the northern Khyber Pakhtunkhwa region where the two governments are in talks to build an oil refinery and power plant, paving the way for the Russia's giant gas company, Gazprom, to enter into negotiations to supply liquid gas to Pakistan.[98]

Shanghai Cooperation Organisation

On June 9th 2017, Pakistan and India became full members of the Shanghai Cooperation Organization, having been observers since 2005.[99]

In this regard, the President of Kazakhstan Nursultan Nazarbayev said: "During our conference in Astana, we can say that our organization will see the light of a new history. This is our organization's last session as a six-party format. As agreed today, we are signing a decision to complete the procedures for accepting India and Pakistan as member states in the Shanghai Cooperation Organization. Accepting new member states will give new and strong impetus for the development of the organization and enhance its international standing."[100]

The most important membership clauses in the Organization stipulate that no border conflicts shall exist between member states and that good neighborliness should prevail.[101] Hence, the

---

people.cn. online. (Retrieved on: 2/6/2017) from: https://bit.ly/2CYkUrH

98   Drazen Jorgic. With gas and diplomacy, Russia embraces Cold War foe Pakistan. Op. cit. from:
https://ara.reuters.com/article/worldNews/idARAKCN1GI1ME

99   Pakistan joins the Shanghai Cooperation Organisation. 26/6/2016. Al-Watan Kuwaiti Newspaper. (Retrieved on: 3/2/2017) from: https://bit.ly/2mvZKed

100   "Shanghai" will be fostered with the adherence of India and Pakistan. 9/6/2017. Sputnik. (Retrieved on: 3/5/2018) from: https://bit.ly/2AUrrBU

101   Dr. Ahmed Ello. November 2009. The Shanghai Pact between alliance of interests and the clash of civilizations. Lebanese Army Magazine. (Retrieved on: 15/9/2017) from: https://bit.ly/2Ezhegc

presence of Pakistan on one hand, and India on the other hand, significantly reduces contradictions that could be exploited by Washington, such as the border disputes between Pakistan and India, and between India and China, which Washington could use to break up the organization or influence the dynamics among its members. The addition of India and Pakistan is directly in the interests of China and Russia, especially with the concerns emanating from countries in the heart of Asia, which may not want United States involvement.

The Trade Corridor and Gwadar Port

Pakistan has successfully implemented an ambitious plan to build an economic corridor with China despite some challenges. China has pledged $57 billion to invest in projects along the China - Pakistan Economic Corridor under the ambitious Belt and Road Project. "We are implementing smoothly and are very pleased with the pace of implementation", Pakistani Planning Minister Ahsan Iqbal told Reuters on the margins of the World Economic Forum in the Chinese city of Dalian. He also mentioned that apart from investments pledged by China, Pakistan will invest about $10 billion. He pointed out that the economic corridor, which will be completed in three phases, no later than 2030, will enhance energy security and infrastructure in Pakistan, which will help them attract more foreign investment.[102]

On another note, analysts suggest that the success of this corridor under construction for about two decades will positively impact future corridors linking India, Bangladesh and Myanmar.[103]

As for the port of Gwadar, China has been granted the privilege of operating the port for forty years starting in 2015. At the time, former Pakistani President, Asif Ali Zardari, said that work in

---

102   The China - Pakistan trade corridor is "going" smoothly. 28/6/2017. Sky News Arabia. (Retrieved on: 19/1/2018) from: https://bit.ly/2mzUKp9

103   Muhammad Amir Rana. 17/5/2015. Economic corridor challenges. Dawn. (Retrieved on: 11/4/2018) from: https://bit.ly/2qWZmtM

Sketch Map of China-Pakistan Railway

Kashi

China

Afghanistan

Iran

China-Pakistan Railway

Pakistan

the Persian Gulf

India

Gwadar Port

The Economic China-Pakistan Trade Corridor

the port will facilitate the transfer of the region's oil to China, making Gwadar the center of trade in the region, bringing together the countries of Central Asia, and will give new impetus to Pakistan - China relations.[104]

The strategic importance of the port of Gwadar lies in its proximity to the Strait of Hormuz (250 miles). In fact, China took advantage of the US refusal of Pakistan's request to develop the port and agreed to cover 79% of the total 500-million-dollar construction cost.[105] According to the large investment agreements signed between the two countries, a network of roads, railways, and pipelines with a length of 3000-km will link the port to the Xinjiang province in western China.[106] Subsequently, many

---

104 China acquires the right to operate Pakistani Gwadar port for 40 years. 5/4/2015. China.org.cn. (Retrieved on: 17/8/2017) from: http://on.china.cn/2mm7lLm

105 Dr. Abdul Azim Mahmoud Hanafi. No Date. Indian concerns regarding the Chinese string of pearls. Al-Metraqa. (Retrieved on: 27/12/2016) from: https://bit.ly/2D4Dz8n

106 Pakistan, a new "Asian Tiger"... with Chinese support. 21/4/2015. Al-Akhbar Lebanese Newspaper. Issue No.: 2571. (Retrieved on: 16/8/2017) from: http://www.al-akhbar.com/node/231001

GCC countries close to Washington, sought to limit the port's activity, as it will reduce their trade and position at the heart of global trade, thereby weakening the allies in the face of China.

Local Currencies adopted in Trade Operations

The former Pakistani minister for financial affairs, Rana Muhammad Afzal Khan, declared that the Central Bank officially approved the use of the Chinese Yuan in bilateral trade between Islam Abad and Beijing. Afzal Khan said: "The State Bank of Pakistan has issued a circular allowing all public and private companies in Pakistan to use the Chinese currency in bilateral trade and investment activities." He mentioned that "this step will reduce Pakistani dependence on the US dollar".[107] This declaration was explosive in the face of Washington which rules the world via the US dollar. Therefore, any trade excluding its currency will weaken its economic status in particular, and its control of the financial market in general. However, the biggest fear lies in the extent to which the dollar, oil, and energy can be decoupled[108], especially with the BRICS Development Bank which favors the use of national currencies. Russia, for example, which has the largest gas reserves in the world, may offer to sell and price energy in rubles. This may also apply to China, which, for a number of reasons, may take similar steps in its dealings, especially since the Chinese Yuan was officially approved as the IMF's main currency in 2016.

Chinese Military Base

China is planning to set up a naval base at the Gwadar port, where China has justified its deployment in the region as necessary to protect its trade, while India and the United States fear China's growing presence in the Arabian - Persian Gulf and the Indian Ocean.[109]

---

107   Pakistan adopts the Chinese Yuan in its bilateral trades. 4/1/2018. Al-Alam News. (Retrieved on: 9/9/2018) from: https://bit.ly/2D4A2H9

108   Jaber Buqshan. 22/9/2018. Russian "Gazprom" is considering to abandon the dollar and link its trade to gold. The New Khalij. (Retrieved on: 25/9/2018) from: https://bit.ly/2xUBmbS

109   Jamal Ismail. 8/1/2018. A Chinese military base sees the light in Pakistan and the "Pentagon" studies retaliations against potential assaults. Al-Hayat

Some analysts believe that China will build its second military base in Pakistan, following that of Djibouti, showcasing more military, economic and political power along strategic sea routes. The facility will be built in Jiwani, a port close to the Iranian border on the Gulf of Oman and is expected to be a joint naval and air facility for Chinese forces. A group of 16 Chinese military officers have already presented a plan to Pakistani officers.[110]

As for military cooperation, the Chinese President Xi Jinping signed a number of agreements during his visit to Pakistan in April 2015, notably the military agreement which stipulates that China supplies Pakistan with eight modern submarines at a cost of 5 billion US dollars.[111]

Abandoning American Weaponry

According to the Pakistani Minister of Defense, "Pakistan's military, historically heavily dependent on US arms and aircraft, may have no choice but to increase purchases from countries like Russia." In addition, both Russia and Pakistan agreed to continue the annual military training exercises which began in 2016. Russia also sold four assault helicopters to Pakistan in addition to Russian engines for the Pakistani JF-17 combat aircrafts which are assembled by the Pakistani army in Pakistani territories.[112]

This major shift in diversifying the source of arms, which Russia strongly supports for several reasons, may be one of the major reasons behind any future war on Islamabad, especially since

Newspaper. (Retrieved on: 16/3/2018) from: https://bit.ly/2mlmQTW

110   China builds a military base in Pakistan. 7/1/2018. Arabic Defense Magazine. (Retrieved on: 9/3/2018) from: https://bit.ly/2EA2NZw

111   Jamal Ismail. 21/4/2015. China seeks to make Pakistan a "Trade Corridor" linking it to the Middle East. Al-Hayat Newspaper. (Retrieved on: 25/12/2017) from: https://bit.ly/2PfNMVG

112   Drazen Jorgic. 6/3/2018. With gas and diplomacy, Russia embraces Cold War foe Pakistan. Op. cit. from: https://ara.reuters.com/article/worldNews/idARAKCN1GI1ME

one of the mainstays of the US economy is the sale of arms, not to mention the ability of the arms exporter to control the power of the State of origin. The United States is one of the elements of Pakistan's power, because it is the source of its arms. This fact makes the latter indirectly dependent on Washington because it will need a lot of materials, equipment, and spare parts, especially in the face of current waves of terrorism.

These and other factors make Pakistan a potential target for Washington, especially as it has a major impact on its policies and influence in the region.

Security Management Strategies for Mega Cities

The management strategy of Mega Cities poses a major challenge in many aspects for the superpowers and large states, especially in terms of security. In the event of a security incident they must be ready for action with specific, predefined plans. Certain economic and administrative capitals of many large and industrial countries have become densely populated, making it quintessential to study this phenomenon. Some reports indicate that cities with high population densities are affected by a variety of threats, for which specific preventative and emergency response systems are required to address and cope with large and small disasters, including natural or technological disasters.[113]

These cities face several important challenges including pollution, waste management, service management, overpopulation, and many more. The focus here will be on the security challenges.

Definition of Mega Cities

According to recent studies, Mega Cities are identified specifically by population size. The classification of megacities varies over time based on the rates of population increase. In other words, when a city's population reaches 10 million and above, it is identified as a Mega City, whereas previous criteria had been only 3.5 million people. It is interesting to note that these cities are not defined by physical size but by the most important measure, population, which is a logical measure. One study indicates that these cities make up 2% of the Earth's surface area and use 75% of the resources. To illustrate, there are 40 megacities with about 300 million people who consume 40% of world resources, 18% of GDP, and produce 10% of total carbon emissions. As a result, such cities have the following key concerns:

---

113   Lewis M. Branscomb. No date. Safety & Security in Megacities. Harvard University. (Retrieved on: 2/3/2018) from: https://bit.ly/2FeGUmq

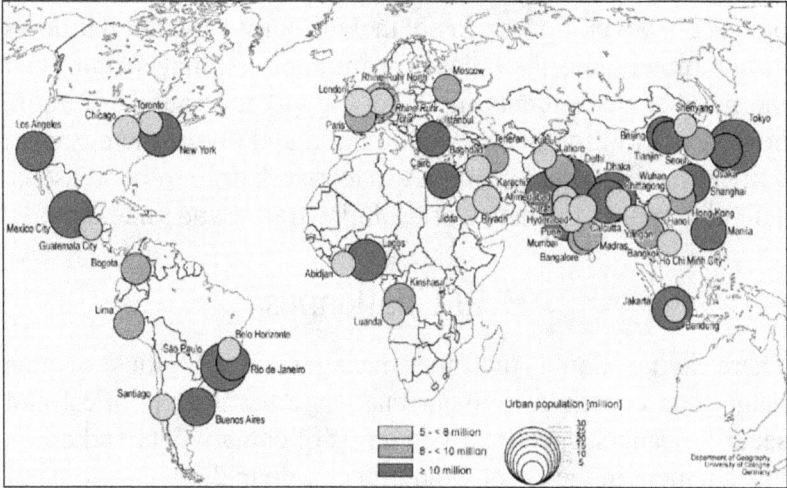

Distribution of megacities according to the UN 2002 map

- Social concerns (including cultural diversity, education, arts, living conditions, transportation, security, healthcare, innovation etc).

- Economic concerns (including labor, unemployment, infrastructure improvement, new technologies, decentralization, wealth redistribution and capital equipment etc).

- Ecological concerns (including energy sources, sustainable development, noise, air and water pollution, traffic congestion, water supply, urban sprawl, urbanization, urban protection, public transport, waste management etc).[114]

- Strategic concerns (including security, protection etc. This issue will be addressed later).

The most prominent megacities are Beijing (China) 21.5 million, Shanghai (China) 24.15 million, Delhi (India) 19 million, Mumbai (India) 19 million, Istanbul (Turkey) 15 million, Moscow (Russia) 12 million, Lagos (Nigeria) 21 million among

---

114   Mega Cities. Jan 2013. EURAMET - European Association of National Metrology Institutes. P: 1.

others. However, figures do not include daily population inflows or commuters into the cities. For instance, estimates claim that the number of residents in Cairo (Egypt) is about 10 million, however, 7 million people commute in and out of the city on a daily basis for work, to complete paperwork or for other reasons. This also applies to many world administrative and trade capitals.

Real Challenges

There is no doubt that the management of cities of this magnitude constitute a major challenge for their political and security leaders, specifically in terms of containment and crises management in the event of natural or human disasters. Some of these events include:

- Natural disasters, such as major fires, destructive earthquakes and volcanic eruptions which severely affect disaster-prone countries. These countries can be identified through historical data, such as the major forest fires that take place in California annually, and such data can be used to design specific population evacuation plans.

- War operations especially since the world today is witnessing a great attraction among the great powers in terms of the reprocessing of smart nuclear weapons, which can erase total populations in seconds. These issues require the creation of private shelters to reduce, and we cannot say to prevent, a lot of losses as well as the ability to deal with such effects in the event they occur, which is also a major challenge that may be equivalent to the event itself. For example, during my visit to Switzerland, the Swiss authorities are forcing homeowners to build a shelter that can contain the number of people equal to the building's residents, so that they can be protected from any military aggression, including nuclear attacks.

- Terrorism has become one of the most important challenges facing large cities. With the development and improved techniques of terrorist operations, these cities are, and will continue to be under huge pressure. There are even rumors circulating that some of these terrorist organizations have the capability to use chemical, biological, and even radioactive weapons in executing their attacks.

- The impact of so-called slums that are made up of poor classes are considered to be the Achilles' heel of large cities and are a reason for increased security concerns, mainly because they contain enclosed areas inaccessible even to state agencies. Consequently, they can form criminal hubs and cause real damage to cities.

- There is no doubt that the demographics within the megacities, especially those based on ethnicity, race, or religion, are a real security threat since they constitute fertile ground for crises ignition and activation. When studying the causes and spread of terrorism, it is evident that there is a direct link between terrorism and demographic distribution. In this context the ruralization of cities has been observed, that is the establishment of cantons within these cities. One of the most prominent examples is the so-called China Towns which are found in a large number of countries and megacities, and agglomerations of dark-skinned populations. The formation of these phenomena could form a pressure, if not a threat, on security especially if these cantons get out of control and start operating organized crime such as arms or drug trafficking.

- The geographical situation of megacities plays an important role in the security challenges they face. For example, the coastal megacities are more prone to threats than the secluded, or inland ones. In the absence of adequate Coast Guard surveillance, the sea turns into a serious security threat as it exposes the city in various ways. In addition, there is a third type of megacity, that is, those cities in which a river or body of water passes through, such as Shanghai, Paris, Cairo, and Istanbul. These may also pose security risks in the absence of specialized authorities to monitor and protect these rivers and bodies of water.

Given the above, several fundamental problems, be they vital or existential, can be identified, especially if the plans put in place do not meet the challenges these cities face. The most prominent of these problems include:

- Impediments to evacuation operations in terms of logistical preparations or safe zones where residents can be transferred in the event of a major event, such as nuclear bombings.

- Chaos among the citizens which could take a heavy toll on the population, resulting in more casualties. Some experts believe that this issue should be analyzed on a wider scale, especially in terms of safety and security, in two respects:

  - "The agencies and officials who are responsible for dealing with earthquakes, fires, power blackouts, and riots must, in most cases, use the same facilities and capabilities for coping with terrorism, and;

  - Only this approach allows an affordable and sustainable effort."[115]

- The prevalence of crime, namely robberies and violence, following security incidents. "The more detailed survey answers by security stakeholders fleshes out their more informed concerns. Organized crime, including by armed gangs, is their biggest challenge — named by 36% of those questioned and by even higher numbers in the Emerging and Transitional cities. Next, a surprising distance behind, comes terrorism (18%), a particular concern in Emerging and Mature cities."[116]

---

115   Lewis M. Branscomb. Safety and Security in Megacities. Op. cit. from: https://bit.ly/2FeGUmq

116   J. Egelhof. No date. Megacity Challenges: A Stakeholder Perspective. GlobeScan & MRC McLean Hazel. Sponsored by: Siemens. P: 51. (Retrieved

In summary, some incidents may overlap. Crime and terrorism, for example, can be intertwined and are not necessarily independent. However, research requirements state that they should be analyzed separately in order to convey each of them clearly and accurately.

Key Solutions

Having identified problems facing megacities, it is necessary to present and define solutions to prevent, or at least cope with, important existential incidents should they happen, bearing in mind global developments and the risks they pose on many levels. Solutions include the following:

- The formation of specialized state bodies that can manage crises through deliberate and predetermined plans designed to deal with many of the crisis scenarios that may occur. This is important in the absence of a comprehensive approach to these threats, especially since some security experts believe that the underlying causes of crime are outside their remit. In response to the question of how best to secure the megacities, "the most popular response is additional officers and law enforcement safety and security capacity (28%), while the third is better preparedness and planning (17%)."[117]

- Dividing megacities into different administrative zones similar to Paris, which is divided into 20 Arrondissements. Each zone has its own municipality and services while still falling under the central Paris administration, which give clear direction on how to develop concrete plans for the distribution of services and forces based on each zone's population. Exceptions are made for areas where there are embassies for instance, as security and stability should be maintained regardless of the number of residents.

on 2/3/2018) from: http://sie.ag/2oCgWzH

117   Ibid. P: 52 – 53.

- Addressing the causes of displacement via equitable development plans for different areas, even though poverty, unemployment, and social issues came last in many statistics. "The survey indicates a greater focus on the threats themselves, rather than underlying causes. The leading ones they named were: crime itself (put first at 24%), corrupt or incompetent law enforcement (15%), poor planning/city management (10%), terrorism (9%), and natural disasters (9%)."[118] For example, paragraph (G) of the preamble to the Lebanese Constitution stipulates the issue of balanced development in terms of population stabilization and remote area development. This is an important and sensitive issue as it is a reflection on general stability and GDP indirectly, as education is provided in a way that increases production and culture and secures the needs of a basic standard of living through the establishment of industrial and commercial facilities. In China, for example, this approach was at the heart of China's strategic development planning for the Xinjiang region when it decided to pass the Silk Road through Xinjiang, making it a huge commercial outlet connecting China to the West, and paving the way for the prosperity of the region as a whole thus raising the quality of life in every respect.

- Activity distribution aimed at reducing the burden on megacities, especially the capitals, through building new administrative cities that mitigate population pressure. This policy was adopted by Egypt when it created the Administrative Capital in an area close to Cairo where official compounds are located. Some countries have built service cities to reduce population pressure by relocating administrative compounds to other regions to reduce the population flow in and out of the main cities. In addition, many countries have established an E-government so that citizens can do most of their transactions from behind the screen without the need to go to government departments in person.

---

118   Ibidem. P: 52.

There is no doubt that this issue will be one of the most serious challenges to face superpowers in the future in terms of stabilizing their influence and status at the global level. Any failure in managing crises will be a black point in their record. An example of this is the disaster that took place in New Orleans following hurricane Katrina, and the inability of the local and Central American authorities to manage the crisis. Their failure negatively affected Washington's international image at the time.

Conflict Between Ethnic Groups

The Buddhist - Islamic Conflict

The media in general and the western media in particular play an important role in the dissemation of information and events. They clearly understand the value of the media as a weapon and have the perfect know-how on how to use and exploit it in favor of the interests of their respective sponsor states.

We all witnessed the events which took place in Myanmar and how the world pictured what happened during the crisis at a much more exaggerated scale. At the same time, the idea of killing one civilian or even an unarmed fighter is not acceptable to anyone of sound mind. However, unfortunately, civilians are only used to fuel wars and are exploited in pre and post war periods.

The use of the phrase Human Rights is being used to conceal the interests of countries and not the reality of the situation. Most states are aware that the use of this argument has become a justification for intervention by major powers in particular, in places where they have not been able to intervene before, or where they want to positively or negatively use them to serve their own interests.

What is happening in Myanmar is the same as what happened in the Levant, but in a different direction. However, the same tools and means were used. Similar events will soon occur in Central Asia using the same means. Two countries are targeted: Russia and China. Both countries consist of different races, religious, and ethnic populations. Moreover, both are surrounded by countries that bear the brunt of their bombings, specifically dating back to the period prior to 1947 when Pakistan was separated from India on religious lines, followed by Bangladesh. There is no reason why the same scenario should not happen again, especially with the development of media tools and the quality of large-scale destructive weapons.

In this regard, this section will focus on China alone since it is currently under the microscope of the West, mainly the United States, after its recent economic success. In fact, the US President Donald Trump said that by 2020 China will surpass the US as the world's largest economy and therefore it should stop or be stopped soon. In both cases, the results will be the same and this is exactly what is happening.

After Washington's siege of Beijing's naval blockade, it sought to close the Chinese Belt crossings, namely the land Silk Road, which links the east and west. In particular, it targeted dual corridors such as the highway that links China to the port of Gwadar in Pakistan, avoiding the Straits of Malacca which is controlled by Washington's allies.

This is where the story of Myanmar and the conflict over the Rakhine state comes into play. If we go back a bit, we see US support for the opposition in Myanmar, by former US President Barack Obama, led by Aung San Suu Kyi, who later became president, and who won the 1991 Nobel Peace Prize. President Obama said that the law which denied Aung San Suu Kyi the presidential nomination was illogical, adding: "I do not understand an item that prevents someone from becoming president because of his children."[1] Furthermore, after having imposed economic sanctions on Myanmar because of the Buddhist - Islamic conflict, former US Secretary of State Rex Tillerson stated that his country was "studying potential economic sanctions to be

---

1   Obama says barring Suu Kyi from Myanmar presidency "doesn't make much sense", 15/11/2014. Annahar Lebanese Newspaper. (Retrieved on: 25/11/2017) from: https://bit.ly/2zIZzVD

imposed on Myanmar due to the Rohingya Crisis."[2] Yet, he had previously stood against this approach and stated that it was still too early to discuss any sanctions.

There are also other opinions on the matter that focus on the fact that China and Myanmar (formerly Burma) are "tightly linked geographically, historically, racially, economically, culturally, and religiously. Also, Beijing and Moscow are both considered to be the main source of support and protection for Burma in the international community. Meanwhile Beijing is the only one able to mitigate international sanctions imposed on it following the use of excessive force by successive Burmese military governments against racial groups and Muslim minorities, where systematic killings, torture, and deportations took place."[3] However, when looking at relations between different countries, they can be measured by their interests as well as their national security. It can be said that China has no interest in triggering conflict along its borders especially since its focus is on managing its Economic Project, The Belt and The Road, as well as lifting the siege imposed on it, which is of top priority for the country.

To further validate the above, analysts see that China "does not hide its support for the Myanmar authorities who, in its opinion, are quelling an unacceptable armed rebel uprising. In so doing, it implements the principles adopted in its relations with other states which stresses the unity and safety of the lands of any state without any foreign interference in its internal affairs. It also emphasizes the importance of negotiations to solve internal crisis of any kind."[4]

---

2   The sanctions imposed by the US on Myanmar following the Rohingya massacres. 22/11/2017. Al-Alam News. (Retrieved on: 19/12/2017) from: https://bit.ly/2zvLHdb

3   Is China playing a role in supporting the Burmese government against the "Rohingya"? 24/11/2017. Alkhaleej Online. (Retrieved on: 25/12/2017) from: https://bit.ly/2iweDv7

4   Mahmoud Rayya. 4/10/2017. The crisis of the Rohingya Muslims: an injustice towards a people with the support of Major Powers. Al-Ahed News. (Retrieved on: 6/1/2018) from: https://bit.ly/2zQ69su

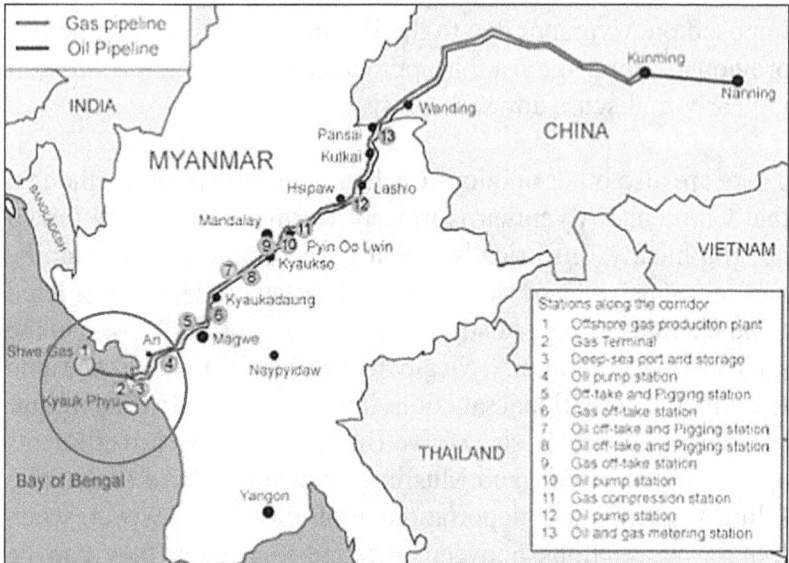

Kyauk Phyu Port - Energy pipelines and oil and gas facilities routes

Referring to the map of the Rakhine state, it is plausible that Rakhine represents about the third of the Myanmar sea front on the Bay of Bengal where China wants to have another double-crossing in Myanmar, similar to that of Gwadar. Therefore, talks about a consortium driven by the Chinese CITIC Group have taken place that will allow it acquire a stake of 70% to 85% of the Kyauk Phyu port (valued at $7.3 billion). However, talks were limited to the state-owned Chinese group and the civil government of Myanmar."[5]

In addition to the port, large pipelines, and gas facilities, are being installed allowing China to import crude oil from the Middle East "into China at about 400 thousand barrels a day. Thus avoiding the sea route passing the American navy controlled the Strait of Malacca where more than 80% oil and gas importations come to China. In this way the time spent on transportation is reduced by 30%, resulting in immense economic benefits for China... as does the 1215 km high speed

---

5   China seeks 85% stake in a strategic port in Myanmar. 5/5/2017. Reuters. (Retrieved on: 9/11/2017) from: https://bit.ly/2A57Pym

railway which links Kyauk Phyu in Myanmar to Kunming located in the central Chinese Yunnan province."[6]

Based on the above, it becomes easy to identify the main reason behind the conflict in Myanmar, or at least a big part of it. Next to Burma is Bangladesh, also on the Chinese Belt, and a country which was indirectly involved in the conflict. The Rohingya are Muslims, and Bangladesh must welcome its brothers in religion. However, it seems that Bangladesh also looked at the situation from a national security perspective and announced that it was unable to host a large number of refugees, except for women, children, and the elderly.[7] After this declaration, and according to the Bangladeshi Minister of Foreign Affairs, Abul Hassan Mahmood Ali, it signed an agreement with Myanmar on November 25th, 2017 stating the return of Rohingya refugees to their countries in two months, provided that the return occurs in a timely manner.[8]

The United Nations High Commissioner for Refugees (UNHCR) published detailed statistics on the Rohingya refugees in Bangladesh and confirmed the presence of approximately 622,000 refugees in the country.[9]

It is important to clarify the recent relations between China and Bangladesh. In a joint press conference, the Chinese Minister of Foreign Affairs, Wang Yi, praised the role Bangladesh played in the trade routes China wanted to open. He stated that his country valued its relationship with Bangladesh, and he placed great importance on their bilateral relations. Besides, Bangladesh is

---

6   Amr Ammar. 9/9/2017. Fraeen News. (Retrieved on: 25/10/2017) from: https://bit.ly/2j6JLke

7   Bangladesh: We will only welcome women and children Rohingya. 13/2/2017. BBC Arabia. (Retrieved on: 26/7/2017) from: http://bbc.in/2AADtVp

8   Bangladesh Foreign Ministry: the return of Rohingya refugees to their country in two months. 25/11/2007. Sputnik. (Retrieved on: 16/12/2017) from: https://bit.ly/2A9w6DN

9   Rohingya in Bangladesh... statistics and figures. 27/11/2017. Sky News Arabia. (Retrieved on: 28/12/2017) from: https://bit.ly/2A8WNbD

"a natural and important partner of the Chinese openness to the west." China is also keen to maintain ongoing high-level visits to reinforce their practical cooperation and to push for the construction of the trade route linking Bangladesh, China, India, and Myanmar.[10]

A quick demographic study of Bangladesh reveals that 90% of its population is Muslims, about 8% are Hindus, in addition to 1% Christians and 1% Buddhist.[11] What if the picture were reversed? What if the Buddhist minority had been persecuted by the Muslims? What would have happened given the West's, mainly Washington's, precedent in using Political Islam to achieve its own objectives and interests? What would prevent them from accelerating this conflict inside China itself through Xinjiang, one of the largest Chinese provinces with a Muslim population exceeding 22 million?

On the other hand, Buddhist - Islamic tensions, similar to those in Myanmar, started making their way through Sri Lanka as extremist Buddhist groups accused Muslims of forcing people to convert to Islamism and of vandalizing Buddhist archaeological sites. Also, at the onset of the crisis, some Buddhist nationalists objected to the presence of asylum seekers coming from Myanmar into their country.[12]

For the record, of Sri Lanka's population of 21 million, 70% are Buddhists compared to only 9% Muslims.[13] This has led analysts to ask questions regarding the link between the events

10   China and Bangladesh push for the trade corridor with Myanmar and India. 21/10/2013. Arabic.people.cn.online. (Retrieved on: 16/3/2018) from: https://bit.ly/2zH352x

11   Bangladesh may exclude Islam as the official state religion. 4/3/2016. Al-Jazeera. (Retrieved on: 13/8/2017) from: https://bit.ly/2n8Gu9q

12   Clashes between Buddhists and Muslims in Sri Lanka. 18/11/2014. Russia Today. (Retrieved on: 17/7/2018) from: https://bit.ly/2zUXvXn

13   Confrontations between Buddhists and Muslims in Sri Lanka. 19/11/2017. Al-Hayat Newspaper. (Retrieved on: 17/7/2018) from: https://bit.ly/2B3snVJ

occurring in both Myanmar and Sri Lanka, despite the 1000 miles that separate them. "It is strange that neither of these countries face threats from armed Muslims, besides, Muslims in both countries... constitute only a small minority."[14]

Based on the above, the following can be concluded:

• Several states which suffer from religious crises were discussed, specifically Buddhist - Islamic ones. However, there are other countries surrounding China that could also be a source of annoyance to Beijing, including Mongolia. Mongolia consists of approximately 3 million people, including 150,000 Muslims[15] mainly living in the provinces of Bayan-Ölgii and Khovd. There is also an extremely critical land route that links China to Russia through Mongolia.

• Observers believe that the crisis was triggered a week before the visit of the Indian Prime Minister, Narendra Modi, to the Chinese city of Xiamen for the BRICS summit. This implies that "the crisis exploded or was intentionally triggered in an attempt to, even partially, distract both leaderships from their increasing mutual cooperation projects in a summit entitled 'Stronger BRICS Partnership for a Brighter Future'... Subsequently, it would not be strange if the oil and gas pipelines in the region experienced attempted sabotage during the next few weeks pretexting rebellion against the government. Exacerbating the conflict and calls for separation will cause delays or cancellations of shipping projects and railways which aim at transforming the coast where the Rohingya live, into a crossing point for Chinese trade into the Indian Port of Kolkata."[16]

---

14   Sri Lanka and Myanmar: The reasons behind renewed violence between Buddhists and Muslims. 19/11/2017. BBC Arabia. (Retrieved on: 25/9/2018) from: http://bbc.in/2hLOjjC

15   Mongolia... 150 thousand Muslims, thirsty for religion. 21/7/2013. Al-Rai Newspaper. (Retrieved on: 25/3/2018) from: https://bit.ly/2Abb6fU

16   Mohamed Sami Mahjub. 16/9/2017. A Turkish Highway to transfer terrorists

- There is nothing that prevents future seditions from being triggered in the region, namely in India and China, between the two largest religions: Hinduism and Buddhism respectively. In fact, Buddhism is the "second oldest religion in India and the fifth in the world in terms of the number of believers… Currently, Buddhists only represent about 1% of the total population in India estimated at about 10 million people, after having been India's official religion for an entire century."[17]

- The West is clearly annoyed by China's expansion in the world. An article in Spiegel Online entitled The New Silk Road focused on this issue. It expressed Europe's annoyance towards Chinese economic and geopolitical ambitions, demanding that Brussels either launch new initiatives to face the Chinese or that it start investing in the same projects.[18]

- These conflicts significantly benefit US interests, as they affect China's economic expansion, and keep American weapons factories in business through future weapon deals needed to nourish the conflict. In this way, the US will also be able to maintain its international status by monopolizing the entire international system.

from Syria to Myanmar. Rose al-Yūsuf Magazine. (Retrieved from: https://bit.ly/2zTzamC

17   The six largest religions in India: A strange mix your Indian friend will never tell you about! No date. m3loma info. (Retrieved on: 15/3/2018) from: https://bit.ly/2iXaiRR

18   What the G7 will do to face the Chinese economic dragon? 25/5/2017. DW. (Retrieved on: 25/4/2018) from: https://bit.ly/2yXlXG8

Private Military Companies - The Example of Russia

The title might seem somewhat exaggerated since we have all heard about security companies. However, taking a closer look at these companies undisputedly reveals that their work is not limited to security work, but also military excellence. In addition to their patrol and security operations, they also undertake real fighting tasks, not only on a defensive level but offensively too.

During the wars of Afghanistan (2001) and Iraq (2003), many heard of Blackwater, the company which was contracted by the American administration. It had "thousands of soldiers dispatched in nine countries, including the USA, with a private fleet of helicopters and artillery, and a unit for spying and surveillance aircraft."[19]

Blackwater was charged with murder and torture, leading the Iraqi government to refuse to renew its work permit after it was confirmed that it had killed Iraqi civilians.[20]

As for Russia, the Russian President, Vladimir Putin, said such companies were "a means of realizing national interests without the direct participation of the state." Russian Deputy Prime Minister, Dmitry Rogozin, said the idea of supporting private military companies was "an idea worthy of consideration".[21]

The State Duma… the Codification of Military Firms

On November 23rd, 2017, the Russian Chief of Staff, Valery

19   Bader Mohamed Bader. 27/9/2007. Blackwater… mercenaries incoming. Al-Jazeera. (Retrieved on: 25/6/2017) from: https://bit.ly/2n60OFh

20   Iraq refuses to renew Blackwater license. 30/1/2009. Al-Sumaria. (Retrieved on: 16/1/2018) from: https://bit.ly/2DDXsTZ

21   Ubaidah Amer. 1/9/2017. The Hybrid war… How Russia operates in Syria? Al-Jazeera. (Retrieved on: 23/9/2017) from: https://bit.ly/2yeh37Q

Gerasimov, declared that Moscow was intending "to withdraw some of its troops from Syria by the end of the year, with armed clashes becoming less frequent and negotiations proceeding toward a resolution of the civil war. To avoid potential security losses or retreats, however, Russia will outsource the work to private military companies with tactical warfare capabilities equivalent to modern militaries."[22]

Consequently, the Russian Parliament, the Duma, began discussions on a draft law for private military companies. That law will specify the "functions of private military companies and the types of services they provide. The law will also ban any modification of sovereign state borders or the overthrow of legitimate governments. It will also ban sabotaging operations and the creation, purchasing, and storage of weapons of mass destruction (WMD). The law will also provide social security for Russian citizens working in these companies."[23] In this regard, the Russian Foreign Minister, Sergey Lavrov, stressed the need to guarantee the rights of individuals working in these companies.[24]

"The law will allow these companies to take part in counter-terrorism operations outside Russia and defend the sovereignty of allied countries from foreign aggression, as well as to protect various installations, including oil and gas fields and railways"[25] said Mikhail Yemelyanov, the first deputy chairman of the State Duma Committee for State Building and Legislation. This confirms that the work of these companies is not limited to security and protection, but extends to military offensives, if necessary.

---

22   Metin Gurcan. 4/12/2017. Private military companies: Moscow's other army in Syria. Al-Monitor. Via The New Khalij. (Retrieved on: 14/3/2018) from: https://bit.ly/2naFBLh

23   Yevgeny Diakonov. 18/1/2018. Russia discusses the legalization of PMCs. Russia Today. (Retrieved on: 6/8/2018) from: https://bit.ly/2DyRQLy

24   Rami Al-Qayluby. 3/8/2017. The Wagner mercenaries… a Russian model in Syria similar to the American Blackwater. Al-Araby Al-Jadeed. (Retrieved on: 25/9/2017) from: https://bit.ly/2BpZqT5

25   Yevgeny Diakonov. Russia discusses the legalization of PMCs. Op. cit. from: https://bit.ly/2DyRQLy

Consequently, Yevgeni Bersinev, editor-in-chief of a private website specialized in private military companies, said: "This draft law is very important. It has become even more controversial following Lavrov's statements. However, the last initiatives of this kind were a failure since some sectors, even within the ruling United Russia Party, refused to legalize the work of military firms. Moreover, relevant parliamentary committees headed by former Ministry of Defense officials also have a position in this regard."[26]

On the other hand, many experts believe that this law contradicts Article 309 of the Russian Criminal Code which "prohibits the recruitment and involvement of mercenaries in armed conflicts".[27] In addition, the 1977 Additional Protocol 1 and the annex to the four Geneva Conventions of 1994, Article 47, paragraph 1 state: "A mercenary shall not have the right to be a combatant or a prisoner of war."[28] However, this does not prevent them from benefitting from Article 75, paragraph 1, of the same protocol, which states that: "In so far as they are affected by a situation referred to in Article 1 of this Protocol, persons who are in the power of a Party to the conflict and who do not benefit from more favourable treatment under the Conventions or under this Protocol shall be treated humanely in all circumstances and shall enjoy, as a minimum, the protection provided by this Article without any adverse distinction based upon race, colour, sex, language, religion or belief, political or other opinion, national or social origin, wealth, birth or other status, or on any other similar criteria. Each Party shall respect the person, honour, convictions and religious practices of all such persons."[29]

---

26 Rami Al-Qayluby. The Wagner mercenaries... a Russian model in Syria similar to the American Blackwater. Op. cit. from: https://bit.ly/2BpZqT5

27 Ibid.

28 Catherine Fallah. June 2006. Active Companies: the Legal status of mercenaries in armed conflicts. Extracts from the International Review of the Red Cross. Volume 88. Issue No.: 863. P: 164. (Retrieved on: 17/11/2017) from: https://bit.ly/2GcvYDJ

29 Ibid. P: 166.

Is Russia Using Mercenaries?

Even now, there are no official statements confirming Moscow's use of private military companies. However, several observers claim that Russia has indeed done so, noting that the first private military company deployed was the Slavonic Corps, fielded by the Turan Security Group, a company established by former members of Russia's Federal Security Service (FSB) commissioned to provide preventive defensive options to protect critical economic assets. The group is formed of elements from Central Asia, identifiable by the group's blue, red, and black patches and flag. In addition to Turan, the Wagner Group, which allegedly conducted security operations in Ukraine[30], is one of the largest Russian firms operating in Syria and is deemed responsible for attracting and recruiting hundreds of Russian mercenary fighters for Moscow in Syria backed by the T-90 battle tank.[31]

Doctrinal Justifications

Some observers say that Moscow uses private military companies within the framework of support forces, the most prominent example was The Weinberger Doctrine, which was established by former Secretary of Defense, Caspar Weinberger, in his famous 1984 speech. Moscow now sees that the recourse to force should be provided at low cost, using mercenaries when needed. In a way, this makes military operations agile and meticulous.[32]

Military and Legal Assessment

Recognizing private military companies has several consquences from many aspects, mainly:

---

30   Metin Gurcan. Private military companies: Moscow's other army in Syria. Op. cit. from: https://bit.ly/2naFBLh

31   Ubaidah Amer. The Hybrid war... How Russia operates in Syria? Op. cit. from: https://bit.ly/2yeh37Q

32   Ibid.

PRIVATE MILITARY COMPANIES IN RUSSIA

	RSB-Group	Antiterror	MAP	MSGroup	Centre R	ATKgroup	SlavCorps	PMC Wagner	E.N.O.T.	Cossacks
PARTICIPATING IN WARS										
UKRAINE ('DPR', 'LPR')	✓	?	✓	?	?	✓	✓	✓	✓	✓
SYRIA	?	✓	?	✓	✓	✓	✓	✓	✓	✓
OTHER CONFLICTS	?	✓	?	✓	✓	?	?	✓	✓	✓

Other Conflicts notes — MAP: IRAQ; MSGroup: PROTECTION OF SEA AND DRILLING TRANSPORTS; Centre R: IRAQ YUGOSLAVIA AFGHANISTAN; E.N.O.T.: TAJIKISTAN NAGORNO-KARABAKH; Cossacks: IRAQ YUGOSLAVIA CAUCASUS AFGHANISTAN GUINEA CHECHNYA

Security & Military Firms in Russia

On the Military Level

- Undoubtedly, since most private military company employees remain anonymous, the use of these companies will reduce the number of official military casualties for many countries, thus allowing governments to avoid being put in an awkward position before their citizens. Kremlin spokesman, Dmitry Peskov, said that "Russian citizens, fighting in Syria, are all volunteers and have no relation to the Ministry of Defense. However, in case they are killed in Syria, they will sometimes receive formal decorations and the schools they trained at will be named after them."[33]

- The use of private military companies realigns the understanding of the Concept of Force between these companies and formal armies. Yevegni Bersinev noted: "Our country is known by a state monopoly on the use of force,

---

33   Mechaal Al-Adawi. 5/8/2017. The Killing institutions "Wagner in the form of Blackwater". Geiroon. (Retrieved on: 17/3/2018) from: https://bit.ly/2DGqljW

in addition to a monopoly on another factor, the distribution of finances. For that reason, I am doubtful that a law will be issued in the near future, even though such companies are already operating in Syria."[34]

- The use of these means reduces a country's financial burden since casualties will receive compensation from their recruiting private military companies rather than from state funds. Thereby removing the financial burden government's face in case of the death of former soldiers - namely compensations, monthly salaries, family securities etc.

- Some observers see that this "progressive strategy is vulnerable at its core as it is based on the use of the least possible number of soldiers on the ground for political purposes. In order to achieve their coercive goals, they will have to use exorbitant state-of-the-art technical capabilities."[35]

- Another important issue to bear in mind is the confidentiality associated with the activities of formal military units. Operations on the ground may require extremely classified military plans which cannot always be disclosed in detail to soldiers because of the sensitive character of certain situations.

- Some military battles require the use of sensitive types of lethal weaponry which cannot be handed over to private military companies, and which need direct army intervention, thus reducing the value of private companies in these situations.

On the Legal Level

- Through the draft law on private military companies, the

34   Rami Al-Qayluby. The Wagner mercenaries... a Russian model in Syria similar to the American Blackwater. Op. cit. from:
      https://bit.ly/2BpZqT5

35   Ubaidah Amer. The Hybrid war... How Russia operates in Syria? Op. cit. from: https://bit.ly/2yeh37Q

Russian legislature seeks to provide legal guarantees for the activities of such companies. However, what is questionable is the control mechanism adopted to keep them in check and prevent them from evading the responsibilities and liabilities imposed by such a law.

- Observers also see that contracting with such companies "does not avail the authorities from the incumbent responsibility in case Russian fighters working for private military companies are killed or taken prisoners in foreign lands as they remain Russian citizens."[36] The state will thus be held accountable for the activities of those companies in case the rules of international law are violated, since they are considered Russian companies, contracting and operating for the Russian state.

- Russia always seeks to apply international law and its rules, especially in terms of state sovereignty and unity, and non-interference in the internal affairs of other states. This is what gives Russia the impetus and momentum to support states with policies inconsistent with those of the United States, providing it with an opportunity to be a reliable ally to them. Hence, the adoption of a law regarding private military companies may raise concerns among those countries regarding Moscow's future policies and make them cautious when dealing with Russia.

---

36   Rami Al-Qayluby. The Wagner mercenaries... a Russian model in Syria similar to the American Blackwater. Op. cit. from: https://bit.ly/2BpZqT5

The Establishment of a European Army

For many reasons based on what was happening in Europe at the time, 23 European countries made the decision to sign an agreement establishing the strategic concept of a unified European self-defense force. The document was signed on November 13th, 2017 and on the eve of the conference of Organization for Security and Co-operation in Europe (OSCE).

This Charter, the Charter of Defense and the Integration of Military Planning, Arms Development and Military Operations (PESCO)[37], aimed to create a new era of military integration in Europe to strengthen the unity of the Union and make it more coherent in dealing with international crises, especially following Brexit.[38] Earlier, a poll by the German magazine Stern showed that 49% of 1,000 respondents supported the proposal to form a European army, while 46% opposed the idea.[39]

Based on the above, many questions arise concerning the reasons behind Europe's establishment of this army, in addition to the positions of the different European countries regarding this, as well as the army's destiny given recent developments on the continent.

Reasons Behind the Establishment of a European Army

There is no doubt that there are many reasons that prompted the leaders of the European Union to think about a European army. Following significant developments in the International system,

37   The European Union lays the foundation of its defense unit. 13/11/2017. DW. (Retrieved on: 26/2/2018) from: https://bit.ly/2kqg427

38   Is Europe able to form a NATO alternative unified army? 14/11/2017. European Center for Counterterrorism and Intelligence Studies. (Retrieved on: 22/4/2018) from: https://bit.ly/2BOXkxt

39   Germans divided on a suggested common EU army. 18/3/2015. Reuters. Prepared by: Amira Fahmi. Edited by: Mohamed Al-Yamani. (Retrieved on: 17/6/2017) from: https://bit.ly/2AxRZMz

solutions for international balance started to see the light in many regional crises, mainly those which reflect the interests of the major powers. In May 2015, Jean-Claude Juncker, President of the European Commission, declared the need to establish a European army, saying that "the existence of a joint EU army would assure the world that there would be no further war among the EU countries."[40]

Many reasons contribute to the creation of such an army, including:

First, the steps taken by the Foreign Policy Coordinator of the European Union, Federica Mogherini, were one of the reasons for what was happening in Europe at the time, namely the British referendum on Brexit. In fact, Britain was itself against creating such an army due to its tight relations with US politics. One of the most important illustrations of such a policy is the 2003 war on Iraq when former British Prime Minister Tony Blair decided to invade Iraq, a decision he apologized for having taken later due to the absence of serious grounds. The British also objected to a similar project in 2011 which explains why the EU and the British government is trying to keep the project under wraps, fearing that it will be exploited by the campaign to get Britain out of the EU.[41]

The most prominent step is the prelude to the March 2017 agreement between the 28 EU member states to establish a joint command and management center for the military training of NATO non-combat troops abroad. However, officials believe the center should be transformed into a European army[42], making the center an introductory step to the establishment of the army.

---

40 Will the European army come into existence? Its creation will allow the old continent to influence the entire world. 10/3/2017. HuffPost Arabi – Anadolu Agency. (Retrieved on: 13/1/2018) from: https://bit.ly/2BFBLhI

41 Top secret European army project... in Britain. 27/5/2016. Sky News Arabia. (Retrieved on: 6/2/2018) from: https://bit.ly/2ATZNsT

42 Will the European army come into existence? Its creation will allow the old continent to influence the entire world. Op. cit. from: https://bit.ly/2BFBLhI

"There is no plan at all to form a European army in the context of a comprehensive strategy, and there is no secret project,"[43] said Mogherini, speaking of a comprehensive strategy for foreign and security policy presented transparently. However, subsequent news reports revealed that Mogherini "spent 18 months preparing for the European Union's common project documents, which will be presented to leaders of European countries for discussion at the EU summit on June 28th, 2016."[44]

Second, when rumors began to circulate about the end of the Syrian crisis, European fears began to grow. Europe is truly fearful of terrorist threats on the continent after the return of European Jihadists to their homeland, especially when terrorist cells were discovered in Europe, and most importantly in Belgium, where the terrorist cells behind the explosions and killings in France were revealed. The former French minister of defense and current Foreign minister, Jean-Yves Le Drian, stated: "About 500 jihadists are there and they will be captured or scattered elsewhere. Their return to France by their own means will be extremely difficult."[45]

Third, the statements made by US President Donald Trump, especially during his presidential campaign and after his election, about the need for real financial participation in the financing of NATO forces, have frightened the Europeans. His adoption of the theory of payment for security and the fear of threatening[46] Europe, from time to time, by withdrawing or redeploying NATO

43   Mogherini no secret EU army plans. 28/5/2016. Al-Alam News. (Retrieved on: 3/2/2018) from: https://bit.ly/2BFBLhI

44   Top secret European army project... in Britain. Op. cit. from: https://bit.ly/2ATZNsT

45   French Defense minister: We have 500 "Jihadists" in Syria and Iraq. 9/12/2017. Asharq Al-Awsat. (Retrieved on: 6/5/2018) from: https://bit.ly/2BpPLAe

46   Many observers say that the US is manipulating Europe and spreading tensions through its contradictory policies towards Europe, namely, the Washington recent threat to Berlin to move the NATO forces from Berlin to Poland. America considers withdrawing its military from Germany to Poland. 30/6/2018. Arabi 21. (Retrieved on: 13/8/2018) from: https://bit.ly/2lWEGN6

forces, has made the Europeans seriously think of the need to find a security solution - a European military[47], particularly with the growing differences between European governments and the US administration.[48] In this framework, the President of the European Commission, Jean-Claude Juncker, called for a unified European army to face the dramatic transformations in Europe following the election of Donald Trump. Many observers see Juncker's statements in the context with reactions that will be studied later.[49]

Fourth, there is a conflict of interest between Washington and Brussels over key issues, not the least of which is disagreement over the Iranian nuclear issue. The EU leadership believes that stability with Iran will solve many of its problems, especially economic ones, since many European companies have rushed to invest in Iran. The administration in Washington put a lot of pressure in many areas, delaying some of the most important business deals, most notably the Airbus deal. The company needed to obtain approval from the US Treasury to sell the aircraft because the US government is responsible for granting these licenses under the

---

47   The French Armed Forces Minister Florence Parly stated that "Uncertainty over US President Donald Trump's commitment to the NATO alliance requires European nations to bolster efforts to forge a common defense policy," adding: "That's why building a common European defense is necessary, in this situation where we don't really know if the assumptions we've lived with for the past 70 years are still valid."
      French Defense Minister: Defense in Europe is necessary in the face of Trump's fluctuations. 21/6/2018. Monte Carlo International. (Retrieved on: 25/8/2018) from: https://bit.ly/2ty4vGZ
      Also see: Macron says Europe can't rely on US for security. 27/8/2018. Al-Manar. (Retrieved on: 14/9/2018) from: http://www.almanar.com.lb/4199131

48   Angela Merkel suddenly declared: "It's no longer the case that the United States will simply just protect us". She called upon the EU to manage its own destiny. At the same time she called for friendly relations with Russia.
      An expert: An extremely dangerous conflict within the NATO. 17/5/2018. Russia Today. (Retrieved on: 24/6/2018) from: https://bit.ly/2rSgVt7

49   Europe considers a unified army away from the NATO, in retaliation for Trump's election. 10/11/2016. Cairo Portal. (Retrieved on: 14/6/2017) from: https://bit.ly/2ABu9he

nuclear agreement.[50] For this reason, the US government managed to delay the process pretexting economic sanctions.

Fifth, following Brexit, some EU member states such as France and Germany have shown a strong desire to build such an army. The analyst Dr. Markus Kaim from the Institute for Political Science in Berlin (SWP)'s noted that "both countries have never wanted to link their national security to the EU as the destiny and future of this European integration project are unpredictable. They have now changed positions and proposed a plan to reinforce joint defense and establish headquarters for the European military staff... it is a six-month roadmap for a new and integrated vision for the EU."[51]

In addition to France and Germany, Hungary also supported the proposal to establish a European army. The Hungarian Prime Minister, Viktor Orbán, said that "we must give priority to security and start building a joint European army". The Czech government also called for former Prime Minister, Bohuslav Sobotka, to "better secure the Schengen zone borders". In his opinion, the priority is not only cooperation against terrorism, but also "to discuss the ability to establish a joint European army". The Polish government walked in its counterparts' footsteps as Poland's conservative former Prime Minister, Beata Szydlo, noted that Europe "needs reforms so that the EU becomes more powerful and developable."[52]

---

50   Farah al-Zaman Shawki. 16/10/2016. Iran complains against the airplane transaction delay and the maintained embargo. Al-Araby Al-Jadeed. (Retrieved on: 11/6/2017) from: https://bit.ly/2AG8rIK

51   Mohamed Khalaf. 20/12/2016. French-German endeavors for a "European Army"... and British concerns on the NATO. Al-Hayat Newspaper. (Retrieved on: 16/2/2018) from: https://bit.ly/2nAqUnd
     Also see: Aachen: Macron and Merkel want to revive Franco-German cooperation. 22/1/2019. Le Monde. (Retrieved on: 15/2/2019) from: https://lemde.fr/2RLNHeF

52   Is Europe able to form a NATO alternative unified army? Op. cit. from: https://bit.ly/2BOXkxt

Political, Legal and Strategic Difficulties

There are many complications associated with such a project, including internal political, legal, and strategic factors, which raises questions regarding the extent to which the countries of the Union are able to implement what has been agreed upon.

The reasons for the difficulties faced by the EU include:

- The Union put itself and its future at risk due to the difficult circumstances it faces, and a series of successive crises on many levels. One of Europe's most prominent issues is the populist tendencies that have begun to emerge, such as the political gains of the French National Front leader Marie Le Pen, in the presidential elections, the arrival of the Alternative Party to the Bundestag, and the emergence of secessionist tendencies within the EU itself, such as in Scotland and Catalonia. In addition, several EU states are experiencing economic crises such as the ongoing Greek debt, the rise in unemployment and low per capita income. Here, important questions arise regarding the role of the EU army in the event of the future disintegration of the European Union.

- There is an absence of a unified European policy on many matters. This is both important and dangerous. With different points of views on the same issue, questions are raised about the concept of European interest that the EU army would protect. For instance, many observers see that the EU states were implicated, "especially Britain, in conflicts they should never get involved in. There were no compelling reasons for involvement apart from solidarity with the US, their biggest ally. Why would British forces join the intervention efforts in Afghanistan? What reason did they have to join the US invasion in Iraq?"[53]

---

53   Hanine Al-Waary. 28/5/2016. The unified army... A European path in maintaining security and evading the American umbrella. Erem News (Retrieved on: 17/4/2018) from: https://bit.ly/2AAWvYI

- It is common knowledge that there are conflicts of interests amongst EU countries themselves, be it on the intra-border level, on the economic level with attempts from certain member states to dominate the internal EU economic market, or on the international level. Most notably, there is a hidden conflict of interest between Germany and France in Mali, and the great scramble for influence on the African continent. This was clearly illustrated in the visits undertaken by French President, Emmanuel Macron, to the African continent in an attempt to restore the Imperial Dream once again.

- Another important factor is the fear that Germany will dominate a European army, especially since it is Europe's most powerful economy and has largely avoided or mitigated the economic crisis that hit the world in 2008. It is able to actually shoulder the financial burden. Many analysts believe Germany's Framework of Nations initiative, which is based on sharing resources with smaller nations in exchange for the use of its forces, would make Germany the most powerful force to improve the level of training of organized forces and raise them to the level of German Army.[54] How can this be the case if a unified European army were created?

- Legal references indicate such an agreement must be made with the consent of EU states in accordance with the founding agreements of the Union, and not through a single decision taken by the President of the Commission.[55] On the other hand, two important positions emerged during the visit of French President, Emmanuel Macron, to Berlin. The first was by German Chancellor, Angela Merkel, who said: "From the German point of view, it is possible to change treaties if that makes sense." The second was by the French president who

---

54   Elizabeth Berro. 14/6/2017. The core of a European army sees the light under Germany's leadership. Al-Hayat Newspaper (Retrieved on: 17/2/2018) from: https://bit.ly/2iGEbWa

55   Europe considers a unified army away from the NATO, in retaliation for Trump's election. Op. cit. from: https://bit.ly/2ABu9he

said there were no taboos with regards to this idea.[56]

- The American element cannot be excluded from the subject. Washington still benefits from being in Europe, even if it has suffered a financial loss. Certainly, this project will not appeal to the United States, and it will try to block it, even to thwart it. Political analyst Andrey Kochkin says the US will never allow the EU to establish its own army so that Washington can keep its control over Europe.[57]

- In addition, Europe is considered the Vital Space of the US towards Russia in the East. Through Europe, Washington can put pressure on Moscow on many issues, particularly those relating to the East European and Middle Eastern countries. Besides, the majority of EU countries are still under the influence of the Marshall Plan, either directly or indirectly.

- Replacing NATO with European troops may be a concern for many European countries bordering Russia, since the features and capabilities of these forces are still unknown, whereas NATO's capabilities are clear and well defined, and it has experience in the many fields in which it has intervened.

- Several reports feared that the future European military would give Russian President, Vladimir Putin, an opportunity to "do whatever he wanted", thus making Russia an ally of the European Union.[58]

---

56   Germany - France: Merkel and Macron ready to change European treaties to reform EU. 16/5/2017. France 24. (Retrieved on: 28/1/2018) from: https://bit.ly/2BjjhYk

57   The European army: a paper tiger. 15/3/2017. Sputnik (Retrieved on: 28/3/2018) from: https://bit.ly/2jkPHao

58   The emergence of a surprising Russian ally. 5/12/2017. Sputnik. (Retrieved on: 5/7/2018) from: https://bit.ly/2BAYIml

The Geopolitics of Energy

The Russian Energy Policy

Controlling the Mediterranean Shores

Russia entering the Iranian nuclear arena was an important source of protection for Iran and a catalyzing force towards the achievement of the Iranian nuclear file, despite the American position on the matter. As with the situation in Syrian, the Iranian issue opened the door for a defense cooperation opportunity with the S-300 missile agreement and the establishment of a regional military understanding in the interest of both parties.

Similarly, Russia and Sudan signed an agreement on the development of a project to build an atomic power station on Sudanese soil. The agreement was signed by Russia's Rusatom Overseas Inc., a subsidiary of the Russian-based firm Rusatom, and the Sudanese Ministry of Water Resources, Irrigation, and Electricity.[1]

This coincided with the invitation of Sudanese President, Omar al-Bashir, to Russia to establish a military base on the Red Sea during his visit to Moscow, citing the issue of US intervention in the region's policy as a pretext. He pointed out that the secession of southern Sudan in 2011 was the result of Washington's policy and American intervention in the Red Sea as a whole.[2]

This simple introduction leads us to the Russian energy policy in

---

1   Russia and Sudan sign an agreement for the development of a nuclear power facility in Sudan. 22/12/2017. Al-Manar. (Retrieved on: 7/6/2018) from: http://www.almanar.com.lb/3116749

2   Will Russia establish its first military base in Africa? 4/12/2017. Sputnik. (Retrieved on: 3/2/2018) from: https://bit.ly/2FnxW3m

the Mediterranean, including oil, gas, and hydroelectric stations. The Mediterranean is the intersection of three continents, thus making it one of the most vital marine areas in the world.

Holding the Turkish vein

Energy and the availability of raw materials are the veins of economic life, especially from a production perspective. The reason for the competition with goods produced by European countries lie in the high production cost that accompanies this process, for example, the high cost of electricity.

Given this, Turkey and Russia signed a bilateral agreement to build the Turk Stream (or the so-called Blue Stream) gas pipeline which will cross the Black Sea, dividing it into two branches: one towards Turkey and the other one towards Europe.

Alexey Miller, the Deputy Chairman of the Board of Directors and the Chairman of the Management Committee of Russian energy company, Gazprom, said the deal would pave the way for the construction of two pipelines across the Black Sea, adding that the annual pumping capacity for each line would be 15.75 billion cubic meters of gas, that is 31 billion cubic meters flowing through these pipelines. Miller pointed out that the agreement aims to build the two lines by 2019. President Putin unveiled the strategic plan at the end of 2014 when Russia abandoned the South Stream project through Bulgaria, noting the problems it may face in the pipeline through Ukraine after the crisis there.[3]

In addition, Gazprom announced that it would increase its natural gas exports to Turkey in the first half of 2017 compared to the same period in 2016. The Russian company said in its statement that the amount of gas exported to Turkey between January and May 2017 increased by 22.6% compared to the same period in 2016. The company increased its total natural gas production in

---

3   Russia and Turkey sign the "Turk Stream" gas pipeline agreement. 10/10/2016.
     Al-Jazeera (Retrieved on: 24/9/2018) from: https://bit.ly/2dsl0uR

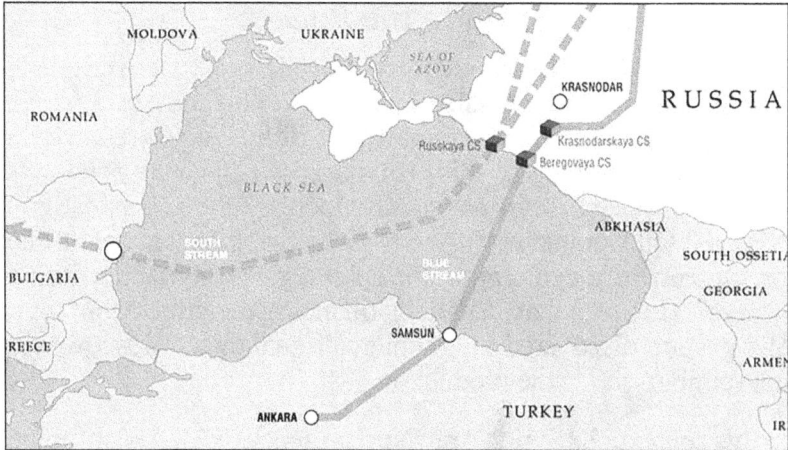

Turk Stream (or Blue Stream) pipeline, alternative to the South Stream through Bulgaria

the first five months by 15.7% compared to the same period in 2016, reaching 198.5 billion cubic meters of gas. The company's total exports increased by 13.3% to 81.2 billion cubic meters compared to the first five months of 2016.[4]

In addition to the gas projects, the Russian president called for the start of construction of the Akkuyu Nuclear Power Plant in Turkey by Russia's Rusatom, based on a previous government agreement on cooperation in the construction and operation of the station near Mersin, Mediterranean, southern Turkey.[5] This is a first-of-its-kind project in Turkey that consists of 4 reactors constructed with 1200 Megawatts production power at a cost of about 20 billion dollars. Therefore, Akkuyu Nuclear Power Plant will be importing natural gas during the next ten years at a cost of 14 billion dollars.[6]

4   Russia increases its gas exportations to Turkey in 2017. 5/6/2017. Al-Arabi Al-Jadeed (Retrieved on: 19/6/2018) from: https://bit.ly/2ANh8iQ

5   Russia starts to implement a nuclear project in Turkey. 11/12/2017. Russia Today (Retrieved on: 14/2/2018) from: https://bit.ly/2B8iAAk

6   Russia starts to implement a nuclear project in Turkey. 1/12/2017. Al-Manar. (Retrieved on: 4/6/2018) from: http://almanar.com.lb/3054445

Syria in the Pocket

In 2013, the Syrian President, Bashar al-Assad's government, granted Russia the concession of drilling for oil and gas in Syrian territorial waters, believed to have one of the largest reserves in the Mediterranean Sea. With Russian financing, the contract's term is 25 years. Information provided by the CEO of Syria National Oil Company Ali Abbas states that this contract "is the first to conclude exploration for oil and gas in Syrian territorial waters". He noted that "Russia is financing the project, but if oil and gas are discovered in commercial quantities, Moscow will get reimbursed for the production cost."[7]

In this context, the Syrian Arab News Agency (SANA) confirmed that the Ministry of Petroleum and Mineral Resources signed the Amrit offshore contract with the Russian company Soyuzneftegaz East Med for Oil exploration, development, and production in the Syrian territorial waters in Block 2. This includes oil exploration on the southern shore of Tartus up to the city of Banias at a depth of 70 km length and 30 km width on average.[8]

Dr. Hayyan Suleiman, an assistant to the Syrian Minister of Electricity and an expert on political economy, said: "I have suggested during several economic forums that in abnormal circumstances, we need typical procedures. States such as Russia and Iran which, like Syria, have lost their citizens' lives are naturally entitled to gain privileges. Therefore, there are consensual contracts with companies from these states which, honestly speaking, must be prioritized over other companies. They have never dealt with Syria on a monetary and economic basis or on a win-lose basis, but with a win-win mindset based on providing Syria with what it needs to secure the expenses of its citizens."[9]

---

7   Russia monopolizes the oil and gas franchise in Syria's sea. 26/12/2013. Al-Yaum. (Retrieved on: 6/2/2018) from:
http://www.alyaum.com/article/3111631

8   Luana Khouri. 8/1/2014. A Russian Company explores oil and gas in Syrian waters for 25 year. Elaph. (Retrieved on: 7/6/2018) from:
http://elaph.com/Web/Economics/2013/12/861438.html

9   Samar Radwan. 27/11/2017. Suleiman: Syria's reconstruction plans set

"Although Moscow's involvement in Syria's maritime energy activities appears to be within technical and commercial frameworks, it will not be seen as well-intentioned," said American author Simon Henderson. "The discovery of natural gas in the eastern Mediterranean, which is huge from a regional perspective, although small from an international perspective, is still able to undermine the dominant position of Russia as a natural gas supplier to Western Europe."[10]

As an addendum to the above, Samir Ruman, an economist, said that one of the reasons for Russia's energy investment in Syria stems from the high cost of the Russian presence in Syria. The Russian United Democratic Party Yabloko, an opposition party, estimated the cost at 140 billion rubles (approximately 2.4 billion dollars). Ruman also noted that "according to Syrian experts, Russia has put its hand on oil and gas in the central region (the central Homs countryside), which is the richest in gas, though incomparable to the oil fields in northeastern Syria controlled by the Syrian Democratic Forces backed by the US. Russia has taken control of the fields of Jihar, Mahr, and Jazal, and seeks to monopolize the rehabilitation of the energy sector, the operation of gas facilities and production of phosphate."[11]

It is possible to say that countries, in general, seek to move the wheel of economy as a priority, but the Syrian issue is a priority for Moscow as if affects Russian in-depth security. Protecting the Warm Water is vital in ensuring there are no negative impacts on Russia coming out of this place in the future.

---

carefully. Sita Institute (Retrieved on: 5/12/2017) from: http://sitainstitute.com/?p=802

10   Simon Henderson. 10/1/2014. The Syrian - Russian offshore gas agreement supports Assad. The Washington Institute. Quoting: Al-Alam News. Arabized by: Bassam Abu Abdullah. (Retrieved on: 7/9/2017) from: http://www.alalam.ir/news/1550245

11   Covering the losses of its military intervention in Syria… Russia targets oil, gas and energy. 29/12/2017. Shaam Network (Retrieved on: 3/2/2018) from: https://bit.ly/2Dv9uve

As for the financing of the Russian army's expenses, Russia will naturally be the first investor. Under the terms of the agreement, Dr. Suleiman pointed out that the Syrian - Russian link is not new but extends to the era of the Soviet Union. This is normal for the two countries, especially with Russia's great contribution in the operations against terrorism, and in preserving the state of Syria and its institutions, most notably its army.

Lebanon in a Battle Between Two Giants

The former Lebanese Minister of Energy and Water, Cesar Abi Khalil, revealed that a consortium of oil and gas companies comprised of Russia's Novatek,[12] France's Total, and the Italian Eni were the only party to bid for oil and gas exploration in Lebanon. Minister Abi Khalil said that the consortium presented two bids for the fourth and ninth blocks, adding that the results of the first licensing round were positive in that Lebanon succeeded in attracting international companies with extensive experience in the development and exploration of oil and gas, and it will enter global markets.[13]

In contrast, the large US embassy project in the Awkar area, northwest of Beirut, is planned to include 174,000 square meters of buildings. According to the embassy's website, the complex will provide a safe, sustainable, and modern platform to support the embassy's staff in representing the US government in Lebanon and in managing daily diplomatic affairs.[14] The building will be completed in 2023 after which, according to many observers, Lebanon will start extracting its energy once the relevant international agreements are reached.

---

12   Russian expert: the future of the Lebanese oil is promising for its closeness to the European market. 1/6/2018. Sputnik. (Retrieved on: 15/8/2018) from: https://bit.ly/2kJYz9X

13   Russia enters Lebanon to explore oil and gas. 14/10/2017. Russia Today. (Retrieved on: 3/6/2018) from: https://bit.ly/2AMgpOS

14   At a cost of a billion dollars… a new American Embassy in Beirut. 24/4/2017. Al-Hurra. (Retrieved on: 9/9/2018) from: http://arbne.ws/2DjuBSF

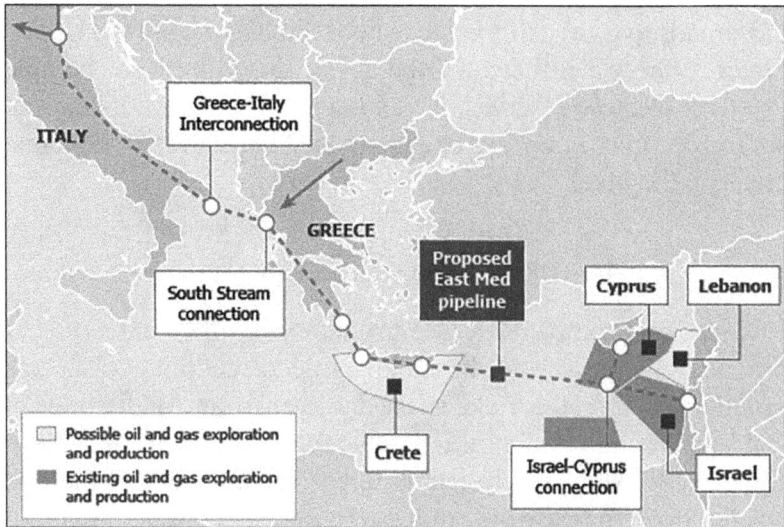

The suggested Trans-Israel pipeline.

Diplomatically speaking, this is only so true. However, politically, an important question arises: Why would the US build one of its largest embassies in Lebanon, facing the Mediterranean? As known to many, Lebanon has been in The Atlantic Orbit since 1985 when the US Marine Corps first set foot in the city of Beirut to prevent the Arab Nasser Empire from expanding into the country.

Another problem facing Lebanon is its inability to link its production to the Trans – Israeli pipeline which goes into Europe (a Mediterranean pipeline project for the transfer of natural gas from Israel to Europe by 2025). The project aims to build a 2,200 km sea pipeline from the gas fields discovered by Israel and Cyprus on the East of the Mediterranean to Greece and Italy, at a cost of up to €6 billion ($6.4 billion).[15] Therefore, Lebanon is forced to link with the Gazprom pipelines which also link the region to Europe.[16] Hence, Lebanon will be at an important

---

15   Europe seeks Israeli gas supplies through the longest sea pipeline. 4/4/2017. Al-Jazeera. (Retrieved on: 9/1/2018) from: https://bit.ly/2AMVprd

16   Russian oil company to operate Tripoli's oil storage. 25/1/2019. The Daily Star. (Retrieved on: 5/3/2019) from: https://bit.ly/2tT7Q3K

crossroads to establish a balance between Russia and the United States. Otherwise, there will be a fear that it will not be able to invest in these reserves, which could save it from its current severe debt crisis on the one hand and the internal economic crisis on the other.

Enter Egypt - The US Ally

Russian oil company Rosneft announced the start of gas production[17] in the Zohr field project, claiming that gas production from the field is the largest in the Mediterranean and will reach up to 28 billion cubic meters per year by 2020.[18] Egypt's Minister of Petroleum, Tareq Al-Malla, stated that the gas field will increase the production of natural gas to 5.5 billion cubic feet per day, adding that "the wells started production at 200 million cubic feet per day and will later increase to 350 million."[19]

Rosneft partnered with other world-renowned companies in this project which aims at developing the largest gas field in the Mediterranean. Stakes will be distributed as follows: 30% for the Russian company, 60% for Italian Eni, and 10% for the UK's British Petroleum.[20] In this context, Osama Kamal, the former Minister of Petroleum, ruled out the idea that political motives or goals were behind this deal, in terms of Russia's relationship with Egypt. As for the Italian Eni, the sale of 30% of the Zohr fields to the Russian company, following the sale of another 10% to British Petroleum, was a way of spreading risk,

17   Rami Aziz. 24/5/2018. Russia's concerning attempts to create influence in Egypt. Washington Institute for Near East Policy. (Retrieved on: 7/6/2018) from: https://bit.ly/2souPnd

18   "Rosneft" declares the start of oil production in the largest Egyptian Mediterranean field. 21/12/2017. Russia Today. (Retrieved on: 9/6/2018) from: https://bit.ly/2EsHZTx

19   Egypt reveals its giant gas reserves in "Zohr". 19/12/2017. Russia Today. (Retrieved on: 17/10/2018) from: https://bit.ly/2CNo0OY

20   Russia purchases a stake in the largest Egyptian gas field in the Mediterranean. 9/10/2017. Youm 7. (Retrieved on: 2/4/2018) from: https://bit.ly/2AMsHXE

especially with low oil prices, and providing liquidity for other investments.[21]

Furthermore, rumors about the possibility of building a Russian military base in Egypt are circulating, or at least the conclusion of a draft agreement allowing Russian warplanes to use Egyptian bases and vice versa[22] for anti-terrorism purposes. These rumors cannot be ruled out because of the importance of Egypt to Moscow's general strategy, especially as the global trend is heading towards the African continent for resources discovered and yet to be discovered.

Director General of Rosatam, Alexey Likhachev, declared that in addition to gas, four nuclear reactors will be built in the city of el-Dabaa in Egypt in 2028 - 2029. Likhachev also said that "key figures show the project cost is $21 billion (85% Russian funding and 15% Egyptian). The four units, are supposed to be completed between 2028 - 2029."[23]

On another note, "there are tensions in European - Turkish and European - Russian relations. Europe is also attempting to diversify their gas resources away from Russia[24] which has succeeded in controlling European energy security using Russian gas supplies as a strategic weapon. This supports Egypt's chances of becoming a center for the transfer of gas from the east Mediterranean to Europe, especially after Washington blocked Russian energy activities while Europe blocked its projects to build new pipelines

21 The reason why Russia purchased 30% of "Zohr" giant gas field. 11/10/2017. Masrawy. (Retrieved on: 6/2/2018) from: https://bit.ly/2CXQPMW

22 A draft agreement... allowing Russian airplanes to use Egyptian bases. 30/11/2017. Al- Arabiya. (Retrieved on: 9/1/2018) from: https://bit.ly/2mesK9m

23 Moscow declares the financial volume of nuclear "el-Dabaa" project in Egypt. 12/12/2017. Russia Today. (Retrieved on: 19/8/2018) from: https://bit.ly/2AMUtTY

24 Egypt: Gas agreement with Cyprus provides energy supplies to Europe. 23/9/2018. The New Khalij. (Retrieved on: 17/10/2018) from: https://bit.ly/2ODrPiW

in response to the growth of European gas needs especially after 2020. It is noteworthy that demand is increasing while there is a decline in domestic production in the Netherlands and Britain, Norwegian production is likely to slow especially after the end of long-term agreements between Norway and Russia."[25] This means that Europe will seek to replace a part of the Russian Gas with the Israeli pipeline going through Egypt.

Back to Libya Through Political Mediation

Libya and the Soviet Union have had a long history since the late President Muammar Gaddafi took over the country. "The Libyan - Soviet economic and trade cooperation developed considerably between 1970 and 1990, during which Russia established a number of power projects in Libya,[26] gas pipelines, and Russian companies drilled hundreds of oil wells."[27]

With the lifting of the ban on Libya, Moscow realized that "it is no longer the only player in the Libyan arena, and that it must enter into fierce competition, especially with Italy, France and Britain which are seeking to extract generous contracts in a country that contains large reserves of oil and gas." With the onset of the *Arab Spring*, Russia lost over $4 billion in contracts, despite being an African and Mediterranean ally. "Russia still puts high stakes on renewing its influence in Libya despite political and military divisions and Western competition. Its approach in relations with Libya is based on its Soviet heritage. Therefore, Russia relies now on the supposedly strong and influential military personalities such as (Field Marshal) Khalifa Haftar."[28]

---

25   Bashir Abdel Fattah. 12/3/2018. Egypt, a regional gas center... opportunities and threats. Al-Hayat Newspaper. (Retrieved on 7/7/2018) from: https://bit.ly/2JNFeyX

26   Libya's National Oil Corporation and Gazprom are discussing the possibility of resuming joint work in the country. 7/10/2018. Sputnik. (Retrieved on: 19/10/2018) from: https://bit.ly/2BY7X3v

27   Russia in Libya... new bargains on old bases. 26/4/2017. Al-Jazeera. (Retrieved on: 6/7/2018) from: https://bit.ly/2CZ8oMA

28   Ibid.

In this context, Russian political analyst Andrei Stepanov said that his country "seeks to preserve the unity and sovereignty of the Libyan territories by bringing together all the parties in a national government with Field Marshal Haftar playing the main role in maintaining the country's security." Russia will "be the guarantor for solving the Libyan crisis in a way that preserves its unity whereas many European countries only care about their interests in Libya."[29]

"With the increase of logistical support to Marshal Haftar's forces and the dispatch of Russian demining specialists, information confirmed the deployment of Russian drones and special forces in Egypt near the Libyan border." This led the Foreign Minister of Malta, George Vella, to say that "Russia, which has funded Haftar, had a strategic interest in establishing a foothold in the central Mediterranean", which some analysts interpret as an "overthrow of the Mediterranean geopolitical system."[30]

In the field of energy, the Libyan National Oil Corporation announced that the gas reserves in its country reached 54.6 trillion cubic meters, thus ranking Libya as the world's 21st largest holder of gas reserves. "It is not a large reserve", the Corporation stated. "We know that for example, Qatar has 24 times the amount of the Libyan gas reserves.[31]"

In addition, Ahmed Maiteeq, Prime Minister of the Libyan consensual government, said that in 2017 Rosneft signed a contract with the Libyan "National Oil Company (NOC), and returned to buy Libyan oil", in the hopes of "expanding the scope of this cooperation. It should be mentioned that Gazprom, through one of its subsidiaries, has established very promising

---

29 A Russian analyst reveals to Sputnik the actions Russia will take in Libya. 15/3/2017. Sputnik. (Retrieved on: 15/8/2018) from: https://bit.ly/2CNdveK

30 Dr. Khattar Abou Diab. 19/3/2017. The Russian intervention in the Libyan crisis. Monte Carlo International. (Retrieved on: 7/1/2018) from: https://bit.ly/2DeuOX0

31 Libyan gas reserved revealed! 28/6/2017. Russia Today. (Retrieved on: 17/6/2018) from: https://bit.ly/2qNWWxN

projects in Libya... Our hopes are that it will be back for implementation later on. The Libyan economy is recovering, including the oil and gas sector."[32]

"We know very well that Russia is one of the most important gas producing countries and will be an important partner for the transfer of Libyan gas through Gazprom's specialized system," said Badad Ganaso, the Minister of Local Government in charge of the Government of National Accord.[33]

In conclusion, the interests of major powers necessitate a military presence to protect these facilities. Within the Mediterranean, Russia now possesses many military bases (in Syria and Cyprus) and military checkpoints (as soon as the protocol is agreed on with Egypt). Therefore, many researchers believe that Russia's presence will be a stabilizing factor in the region. Countries have been treated respectfully in terms of their rights and interests on a win-win basis, so as to fill the American vacuum that was based on the principle of dependence and domination.

American Gas Filling the Energy Gap

The real geo-economic battle between Russia and the United States seems to have already started, as much information suggests that the United States will dominate clean energy in the world, that is, gas.[34]

The US starting its gas exportation is a provocative factor for Russia as gas would not only pour money into the Treasury, but

---

32 Maiteeq: The Libyan economy in recovery and Russian companies must implement their former projects. 15/9/2017. Russia Today. (Retrieved on: 6/1/2018) from: https://bit.ly/2D0BnyS

33 Samar Radwan. 20/12/2017. Minister Ganaso: The "Libyan gas" is an international fortune to be invested. Sita Institute. (Retrieved on 17/6/2018) from: http://sitainstitute.com/?p=1178

34 The American Petroleum Institute estimated that the liquefied natural gas exportations will add to the American economy 50 to 73 billion dollars between 2017 and 2040. See: Gas exportations will add 73 billion dollars to the US economy. 6/10/2017. Al-Araby Al-Jadeed. (Retrieved on: 25/6/2018) from: https://bit.ly/2tih3lM

would also be a geo-strategic weapon, by which Moscow currently fosters its world influence. With its specialized companies in the field, Russia will be able to control large geographic lands, and will be the backbone of new clean energy.[35]

Therefore, the US President Donald Trump's administration noted that "it intends to guarantee justice and balance to the energy market, offering American gas to Europe and Asia. It pointed to the importance of reducing the so-called distorted power of players like Russia and OPEC."[36]

Exploration and Infrastructure

In defiance of former President Barack Obama's decisions on environmental protection, the Trump administration announced that the US coastal waters were almost completely open for oil and gas exploration at sea, including off the coast of California, Florida, and the Arctic. It will be implemented in 2019 under a new five-year Ocean Energy Management Program. It covers 90% of the US coastal waters that have 98% of unexploited oil and gas reserves. In this context, the American secretary of Natural Resources, Ryan Zinke, confirmed that "the US authorities intend to grant 47 exploration licenses for the 5-year project [as] the current provisions allow the exploration of only 6% of relevant offshore areas." 19 of these licenses will be allocated to the Alaskan coasts, 7 for the Pacific, 12 for the Gulf of Mexico and 9 for the Atlantic.[37] In addition, estimates show that liquefied natural gas is also found in Texas and Louisiana, "leading to huge production abundance and to the reduction of the world energy prices."[38]

35   The Russian Embassy in Washington: the United States imposes its liquefied gas on Europe. 24/5/2018. Russia Today. (Retrieved on: 13/8/2018) from: https://bit.ly/2ko3ZXZ

36   Moscow warns Europe against relying on US gas. 10/2/2018. Asharq Al-Awsat. Issue No.: 14319. (Retrieved on: 3/7/2018) from: https://bit.ly/2EiRA3Q

37   Trump's administration allows oil and gas exploration in US coasts. 6/1/2018. Al-Hayat Newspaper. (Retrieved on: 14/3/2018) from: https://bit.ly/2EN4cQ2

38   Clifford Crouch. 31/10/2017. The US wealth in liquefied natural gas threatens

In addition, many economic sources point out that the majority of "long-term natural gas contracts lasted 20 years, and for the most part, will end between 2018 and 2020. Therefore, the US is trying to reshape the long-established world trade pattern", especially given that the world's natural gas market will be reshaped once again in 2018. In this context, Kathleen Eisbrenner, CEO of Next Decade, a company which seeks to build an exportation station in Texas and an importation facility in Ireland, says that "ending liquefied natural gas contracts is a huge opportunity", adding "the next year (2018) will be pivotal."[39]

In preparation for this new situation, the United States is seeking to increase work in its gas sector infrastructure, where many researchers believe that the amount of US exports could be greater than it would be without the constraints of infrastructure. There is no port in the United States that can handle the giant oil tankers.[40] The US only has "one active harbor for the exportation of liquefied natural gas, 6 others ports under construction and it projects to build 30 ports in the future."[41]

The US Message to Europe

The US has already started to supply Europe[42] with gas. Poland was one of the first countries to receive American gas shipments. The Polish Foreign Minister, Witold Waszczykowski, said that his country received one or two liquefied natural gas carriers in an attempt to study the feasibility of importing gas from US. He

the world's energy. Asharq Al-Awsat. Issue No.: 14217 (Retrieved on: 12/12/2017) from: https://bit.ly/2H2GY6N

39   Bloomberg: America hits Qatar and Russia at the core through gas. 2/11/2017. Al-Masry Al-Youm. (Retrieved on: 17/2/2018) from: https://bit.ly/2nZB6T7

40   Henning Gloystein. 11/2/2018. How soaring U.S. oil exports to China are transforming the global oil game. Reuters. (Retrieved on: 25/8/2018) from: https://bit.ly/2EiO1uu

41   America plans to dethrone Qatar in liquefied gas by 2024. 10/6/2017. TRT Arabia. (Retrieved on: 9/8/2018) from: https://bit.ly/2H5CjRv

42   Europe imports more US natural gas. 9/8/2018. Emirates News Agency - WAM. (Retrieved on: 16/9/2018) from: http://wam.ae/ar/details/1395302702930

confirmed that his country has not yet taken any final decisions with regard to purchasing US gas, since they are still waiting for the US conditions regarding the supply of gas on a permanent basis.[43]

In return, former secretary of state, Rex W. Tillerson, confirmed that his country "will support Poland's efforts to diversify energy sources, including liquefied natural gas from the US." Referring to the Nord Stream - 2 Project, the Polish Foreign Minister, Jacek Czaputowicz, said: "Poland provided the US with concrete evidence regarding this project, implying it will reinforce geopolitical tensions in the region."[44]

The United States has also supplied gas to Lithuania for the first time, according to Foreign Office spokeswoman, Heather Nauert. "The supply of liquefied natural gas to Lithuania is another step towards controlling the European market with crude oil, which has become available in America through new extraction methods."[45] It is noteworthy that Lithuania became "the first former Soviet republic to import liquefied natural gas shipments from the United States in August 2017." The shipment came to Lithuania "one month after Poland became the first Eastern European state to import natural gas from the US."[46] In addition, the United States also seeks to supply Eastern Europe with gas, which might be interpreted as a clear political message towards Moscow, has been the dominating entity and only supplier in these markets.[47]

---

43   Fred Geerley. 7/8/2017. The Gas war... Poland sets a condition for purchasing the blue fuel from the US. Russia Today. (Retrieved on: 19/2/2018) from: https://bit.ly/2Eg9yzT

44   Washington instigates Europe against a Russian gas project. 27/1/2018. Al-Watan. (Retrieved on: 27/5/2018) from: https://bit.ly/2G11xPN

45   Washington: Lithuania acquires American liquefied gas for the first time. 24/8/2017. Masrawy. (Retrieved on: 13/9/2018) from: https://bit.ly/2EBgefc

46   Clifford Crouch. The US wealth in liquefied natural gas threatens the world's energy. Op. cit. from: https://bit.ly/2H2GY6N

47   Washington: Lithuania acquires American liquefied gas for the first time. Op. cit. from: https://bit.ly/2EBgefc

The United States opposes the Blue Stream project through Turkey and the Nord Stream – 2 route through Germany[48], which they consider dangerous and undesirable. In addition, Washington put diplomatic pressure[49] to lobby the Balkan states in general and Greece in particular to prevent Russia's exportation projects that are attempting to provide some European countries such as Italy, the Netherlands and the United Kingdom with liquefied natural gas. On the other hand, experts agree that the Blue Stream line is no longer effective, while the struggle has begun to complete the same line towards Europe through Turkey.[50]

As for the Nord Stream – 2, despite Germany's objection, the United States, together with the European Union is attempting to halt the project as it will put the continent under the mercy of Moscow, which is trying to acquire all necessary permits to start extending the pipeline across the Baltic Sea. The Chief Executive Manager of the company, Matthias A. Warnig, said that his main goal is "to ensure the construction (of the pipeline) in 2018, especially since we have met all technical requirements and we will mobilize our partners to launch the project. We have just gotten permission from Germany and will soon acquire licenses from Sweden. Overall, we expect the completion of the licenses in the coming months." He noted that "Washington is looking at the project negatively, while it barely understands the European energy market and is keen to highlight the threats coming from Russia."[51]

48   Fred Geerley. 15/5/2018. The US threatens the "Nord Stream" with sanctions. Russia Today. (Retrieved on: 27/9/018) from: https://bit.ly/2INeEsP

49   "Foreign Policy" magazine stated that the US President Donald Trump's administration is close to imposing sanctions on German and European companies involved with the construction of the Russian gas pipeline "Nord Stream - 2". For more details, see: Olga Rudkovskaya. 2/6/2018. Washington is planning to impose sanctions on European companies because of the Russian Gas. Russia Today. (Retrieved on: 14/8/2018) from: https://bit.ly/2Jo5zXO

50   The United States tries to cut Russian gas pipelines in Europe. 6/12/2017. Russia Today. (Retrieved on: 14/3/2018) from: https://bit.ly/2EVvjpV

51   Fred Geerley. 9/2/2018. The "Nord Stream – 2" sees the light. Russia Today. (Retrieved on: 7/11/2018) from: https://bit.ly/2G5aBTZ

Here, it should be noted that the Finnish government granted one of the necessary approvals for the extension of the Nord Stream – 2 pipeline through its economic waters. The approval of the Finnish Government was accompanied by specific conditions to be complied with by project operators, including the need to observe the principle of "caution, prevention and reduction of accidents and damage" during construction, taking into account the specificity of the Baltic Sea and other projects in the Finnish territorial waters.[52]

On the African side, the United States is trying to coax Algeria, which is close to Russia, where it expressed its desire to conclude a partnership agreement with it to "supply gas to European countries, especially Eastern European countries, in an attempt to break the monopoly imposed by Russian energy companies as Algeria is a huge energy supplier for Europe. We congratulate it on being a reliable partner that helps the continent diversify its supplies."[53] Abdelmoumen Ould Kaddour, Chief Executive Officer of the Algerian national energy company, Sonatrach, said that "Algeria will get more ships to transport gas to Asia as it looks to increase sales to that region," adding that "there is fierce competition in the gas market between Russia and the United States. Europe is our traditional customer but we also need to win Asian markets to sell our gas."[54]

In addition, Morocco and Nigeria signed a huge agreement to build a 5,660-km gas pipeline linking the two countries across the Atlantic in West Africa, a pipeline used since 2010 linking Nigeria, Benin, Togo, and Ghana. Officials from both countries

---

52 Finland grants its approval to the Russian gas project "Nord Stream – 2".
    5/4/2018. Russia Today. (Retrieved on: 7/10/2018) from:
    https://bit.ly/2Jy9AFw

53 An American official urges Algeria to increase its exportations towards
    Eastern European states. 30/1/2018. Annasr Online. (Retrieved on: 17/3/2018)
    from: https://bit.ly/2snbHID

54 Hassy Massoud. 12/2/2018. Algerian Sonatrach wants more ships to foster gas
    sales to Asia. Reuters. (Retrieved on: 7/6/2018) from:
    https://bit.ly/2Cfjacn)

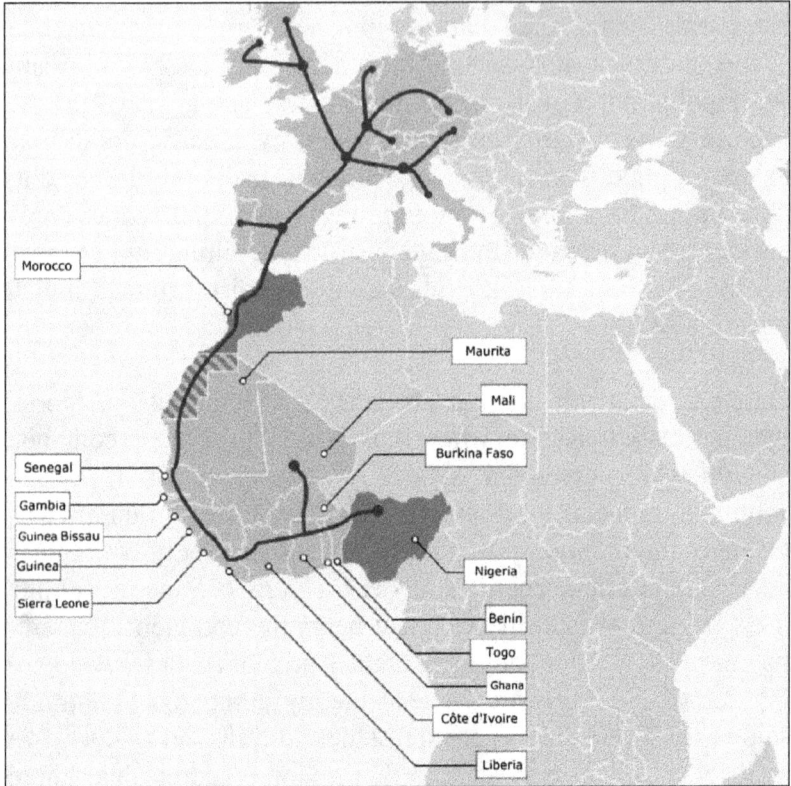

Nigeria-Morocco gas pipeline

stressed that "For economic, political, legal and security reasons, the choice was made on a combined onshore and offshore route."[55] Not only is this project important because it could supply Europe with gas for the next 25 years, but it is also a blow to Russia in terms of energy, especially since the Kingdom of Morocco is a US ally. Also, this downplayed the 4128-km NIGAL pipeline which comes from Nigeria to Europe through Niger and Algeria, and which is financially covered by Russia's Gazprom and the European Central Bank.[56]

---

55   Morocco and Nigeria sign a huge gas pipeline project. 10/6/2018. DW. (Retrieved on: 25/6/2018) from: https://bit.ly/2K9LfJX

56   Alwan N. Amin Eddine. 2015. Globalization and Sovereignty in International and Regional Relations. Dar Abaad. Beirut – Lebanon. 1st Edition. P: 157.

The Middle East

The UAE Minister of Energy and Industry, Suhail Mohammed Faraj Al-Mazroui, said that American liquefied gas may find a promising market in the UAE and GCC countries as the US possesses huge amounts of gas and US companies are starting to market themselves in the UAE and the GCC. He pointed to a huge opportunity for cooperation with the US in this field if its companies offered competitive rates. Minister Al-Mazrouei stressed that his country is at the forefront in terms of carbon sequestration and carbon sequestration technology that meet the 2050 Energy Strategy and reduce carbon dioxide emissions by 70%. This contributes to achieving innovation and pioneering national carbon emission indicators to transform challenges into opportunities and maintain quality.[57] The use of gas as a source of energy is particularly important in light of the worsening political crisis with Qatar and the growing fears regarding gas supplies from the Dolphin Gas Pipeline.

China and the Far East... A Strategic Goal

Some reports indicate that the United States exports 330,000 tons per year, all of which go to Japan and Taiwan exclusively[58], a sign of increasing its influence on the East Asian economy. The United States is also trying to enter the Chinese market through gas, where "US oil shipments to China, establishing trade between the world's most powerful states which did not exist until 2016. This helps Washington in its efforts to reduce the huge trade deficit with Beijing... (since) raw material shipments from America to China started from scratch before 2016 and reached a record of 400 thousand barrels a day in January 2018 at a cost of one billion dollars. In addition, China also received

---

57   US gas may find a promising market in the UAE and Gulf countries. 6/12/2017. Arabian Business.(Retrieved on: 7/11/2018) from: https://bit.ly/2G3FJD3

58   America plans to dethrone Qatar in liquefied gas by 2024. Op. cit. from: https://bit.ly/2H5CjRv

a half million tons of American liquefied natural gas at a cost of 300 million dollars in January 2018."[59]

In a very important reference, the US energy company, Jenny Energy, announced the start of export of liquefied natural gas to India. The first marine carrier[60] carrying the gas to India sailed on March 5th, 2018 from the port of Sabine Pass - Louisiana, in the southern United States. The company says it will export 3.5 million tons per year of liquefied natural gas to India, according to a 20-year agreement signed with India's largest natural gas company, Gail India, where some observers confirm that the export agreement contributed to the establishment of good relations between the two companies in the long run.[61] Based on these factors, the following conclusions can be summarized as follows:

• Washington is trying to negatively take advantage of the history in Russian - Japanese relations. To date there has been no official agreement that formally ends the 1945 war between the two countries; however, Tokyo is making huge efforts with Moscow in this matter because of their economic interests on many levels.

• The United States continues to increase Taiwan's strength in the face of China in tackling any future negative repercussions. The Island is considered a natural ally of Washington in the face of Beijing and away from the Russia - China bloc, particularly Russian gas, and it is a service to Washington's strategic interests.

---

59 Henning Gloystein. How soaring U.S. oil exports to China are transforming the global oil game. Op. cit. from: https://bit.ly/2EiO1uu

60 India sought to purchase additional amounts of Iranian oil to be delivered on June 2018, though America declared it will impose new economic sanctions on Iran in May. For more details, see: Despite American sanctions, the second biggest Iranian oil importer takes this measure. 2/6/2018. Sputnik. (Retrieved on: 13/9/2018) from: https://bit.ly/2sH5ggz

61 An American company starts exporting liquefied natural gas to India. 6/3/2018. Anadolu Agency. (Retrieved on: 10/7/2018) from: https://bit.ly/2HSSEsW

- The stated goal of the policy, exporting gas to Beijing, is to reduce the trade deficit between the two countries, especially after President Donald Trump took office. Official Chinese figures showed a decrease in the deficit between the countries from $25.55 billion in December 2017 to $21.895 billion in January 2018. Based on the average quantities during this period, US oil and gas sales to China could be estimated at about $10 billion a year.[62]

- It seems that Washington wants to acquire the World's factory, that is China, before the implementation of the Siberian Power project which will supply Beijing and New Delhi[63] with gas especially after the global trend towards clean energy to reduce toxic emissions. In this regard, Gazprom confirmed in March 2016 that the pipeline will start operating as of May 2019.[64] In addition, a refinery manager at Chinese oil giant Sinopec said: "Sinopec is looking to buy more US crude this year (2018)", adding "We see US crude as a complement to our large crude base from the Middle East and Russia."[65]

- America is concerned with the expansion of Russian gas projects to other countries in the region, placing them at the mercy of Russian energy. For example, Moscow and Tokyo deliberated a gas pipeline project heading to Tokyo through the Sakhalin Island, where Naokazu Takemoto, a member of the ruling Liberal Democratic Party, said he wanted "to draw attention to the government's importance for this project, which has been under way for many years. Construction of the Sakhalin gas pipeline will contribute effectively to the

---

62   Henning Gloystein. How soaring U.S. oil exports to China are transforming the global oil game. Op. cit. from: https://bit.ly/2EiO1uu

63   For this reason, the US is attempting to cut Russia's access to that area. In this regards see: An American company starts exporting liquefied natural gas to India. Op. cit. from: https://bit.ly/2HSSEsW

64   Ali Youssef. 14/5/2017. The gas of Russia to China via the "Power of Siberia". Russia Today. (Retrieved on: 17/9/2018) from: https://bit.ly/2HgQcMR

65   Henning Gloystein. How soaring U.S. oil exports to China are transforming the global oil game. Op. cit. from: https://bit.ly/2EiO1uu

economic growth strategy currently being implemented in Japan, including plans to rebuild the country's energy system, and reconstruction of areas affected by natural disasters."[66] This 1350-km pipeline supplies Japan with gas through a pipeline extending to Wladiwostok, Russia, for exportation to Ibaraki, in north east Tokyo.[67] In 2016, Japan began to receive Russian gas shipments through the Sakhalin - 1 and Sakhalin - 2 projects. Russian President, Vladimir Putin, confirmed that 70% of the liquid natural gas produced on Sakhalin Island goes to the Japanese market across these two lines.[68]

Using Friends to Face Foes

Some experts believe that the United States plans to occupy the throne of gas by 2024, through the export of 300 million tons of liquefied gas annually, which is the closest competitor to Qatar in this sector.[69] In addition, Amin H. Nasser, chief executive of Saudi Aramco, said: "We have no concern at all about increasing US exports, our credibility as a supplier is unmatched, and we have the largest customer base with long-term sales agreements."[70]

Based on the above, the following can be concluded:

• The United States is one of the most important strategic planners. Talk about the end of energy contracts in a relatively recent period will make it a fierce aggressor seeking to occupy world markets.

---

66   Japanese deputies call for the construction of gas pipelines from Russian Sakhalin to Tokyo. 9/6/2014. Al-Aahed News. (Retrieved on: 5/3/2018) from: https://bit.ly/2BxgHNO

67   Experts: Japan towards importing Russian gas soon. 2/6/2014. Masr Al-Arabia. (Retrieved on: 7/3/2018) from: https://bit.ly/2GhBMLa

68   Putin studies means of supplying Japan with Russian natural gas. 2/9/2016. Sout Al- Omma. (Retrieved on: 7/3/2018) from: https://bit.ly/2EuU8bg

69   America plans to dethrone Qatar in liquefied gas by 2024. Op. cit. from: https://bit.ly/2H5CjRv

70   Henning Gloystein. How soaring U.S. oil exports to China are transforming the global oil game. Op. cit. from: https://bit.ly/2EiO1uu

- Through its allies, the US can access many international markets, such as Saudi Aramco for example. After invading the market, the United States can pressure its allies to leave the market so it can fill it with its exports later.[71]

- Writers note that the US lobbied Qatar to increase its production of liquefied natural gas, making the latter produce 100 million instead of 77 million tons a year as an alternative to the Russian gas supply to Europe. The US also lobbied Turkey to prevent Russia from using Turkish land to reach the European continent.[72] Thus, when US infrastructure is equipped and the capacity to supply the Old Continent is met, there will be no objection to Washington pressing Doha to decrease production again.

- Distributing energy to Eastern Europe's former communist states will highly impact the halt of the Russian expansion in Eastern Europe, according to the American understanding. The need for gas in industry and heating will turn the US into a strategic need.

- The extension of NATO's energy will help stop Russia's appeasement and even confront it if necessary, especially as the military expansion of the alliance increases, following the launch of the Schengen Military Initiative, which helps speed the transfer of military forces among the NATO countries.[73]

---

71 Azerbaijan opens a pipeline project towards Turkey and seeks to reach Europe. 29/5/2018. Reuters. (Retrieved on: 11/6/2018) from: https://bit.ly/2J5bCNt Also see: The "Southern Gas Corridor" aims to transport 10 billion cubic meters of Azerbaijani gas to Europe via Georgia and Turkey. See: Finding a new route to Europe... Putin rejoices! 29/5/2018. Sputnik. (Retrieved on: 15/8/2018) from: https://bit.ly/2LOG7Jc

72 Moataz Ali. 5/8/2017. Gas the secret word... encircling Qatar is the American weapon to defeat Erdoğan and Putin. Sasa Post. (Retrieved on: 18/3/2018) from: https://bit.ly/2nSwzmp

73 Asia Atrous. 7/12/2017. NATO, terrorism and seeking a "military Schengen", when Tillerson chooses evasion rather than confrontation. Rai Al-Youm. (Retrieved on: 15/6/2018) from: https://bit.ly/2Ez1crq

Concocting Crises

There is no doubt that the United States is ingenious in creating crises, especially since it has effective media, military power and political influence. After observing global events and linking them to gas, the following can be observed:

- It is clear that the US sanctions on Russia are, even indirectly, linked to this issue. The Russian Minister of Energy, Alexander Novak, sees that "the attempts to halt the Nord Stream – 2 is part of unlawful competition practices by potential suppliers of liquefied natural gas, which is more expensive compared to natural gas passing through pipelines. These politically motivated economic constraints make energy resources in the market ultimately more expensive."[74]

- The recent escalating situation between Sweden and Russia is not a coincidence. When Sweden declares that there is a Russian threat and starts distributing pamphlets to its citizens that contain instructions in case of war, it cannot be seen as a passing act. Through this gas war, it can be observed that Russia is attempting to acquire licenses from Sweden, extend the Nord Stream – 2 pipeline in the Baltic Sea, and this tension may be behind the suspension of such a project.

- The situation is still tense in Ukraine, even increasing, especially with Ukrainian measures aimed at entering into a military conflict with Russia, staged in the province of the Donbass. What is concerning is the gas pipelines that go through Ukraine, and the possibility of cutting them to pressure Europe into importing US gas.

- The US sanctions on Russia also contributed to significant damage to some European countries. With respect to gas,

---

74   David Sheppard and Henry Foy. 5/8/2017. The gas market... a Russian - American battle where Europe wins. Al-Eqtisadiah. (Retrieved on: 19/8/2019) from: https://bit.ly/2BojrNt

Russia stopped the South Stream and replaced it with the Blue Stream, which crosses Turkey, which deprived Hungary of the annual financial revenues estimated at $400 million, in addition to the use of Russian gas.

- The US escalation in Syria, the military presence in the North[75] and the support of the Kurds for the establishment of a state, comes as Washington wants its share of the Syrian Cake[76] of gas. In these terms, President Trump underlined the huge mistake committed by Obama's administration by withdrawing from Iraq.

- As far as Iran is concerned, the issue is much deeper than gas, and cutting pipelines will halt treasury revenues. In addition, this product could be a rival to the United States even among its allies, especially Pakistan, where it benefits from gas pipelines crossing its territories.

- Many researchers believe that the issue of Myanmar is not entirely out of the question. Despite being a crisis that stifles China in terms of energy, it may also be a point of entry into the Chinese market in a bigger and more effective way.

Major Challenges for Washington

In addition to infrastructure, there are many challenges that stand in the way of the US in this sector, mainly:

Pricing Issues

Some information points to the fact that Washington may benefit from, among other things, "the end of most long-term liquefied

---

75 Megan Specia. 16/1/2019. The Planned U.S. Troop Withdrawal From Syria: Here's the Latest. The New York Times. (Retrieved on: 12/3/2019) from: https://nyti.ms/2RRMja7

76 Syria, the world's third gas producer... Trump wants a part of the Syrian gas "cake". 10/5/2017. Al-Alam News. (Retrieved on: 5/4/2018) from: https://bit.ly/2EN9Str

natural gas contracts, rising US gas supplies, increasing demand in Europe and Asia, the geopolitical tensions surrounding Qatar and Russia, the world's largest gas suppliers, while bearing in mind security and stability are extremely important factors in the gas market."[77]

These factors are also supported with data indicating that Russia has been forced to "reduce the price of gas exported to Europe in an attempt to reduce the European thirst for US gas. These efforts entailed huge revenue losses for Russian companies and the expansion of liquefied natural gas facilities in the North Pole became economically useless."[78]

"Compelling Russia to compete in Europe's most competitive gas markets and giving European consumers alternative sources of energy supplies is weakening Russia's geopolitical influence in Europe," said Jason Bordoff, former energy adviser to the Obama administration and current director of Columbia University's Center for Global Energy Policy. "Russian geopolitics within Europe and the transformation of the United States into one of the world's largest natural gas exporters has enormous economic, environmental and geopolitical effects on Washington."[79]

Bordoff also says that Gazprom has to choose: either to compete in the market and defend its market share, or to decrease its supply to keep the prices high. If it chooses the first option, "then it will need to accept a price war that could damage its revenues even if it can sustain increased sales in an energy-hungry region."[80] However, choosing the second option will also play in favor of Russia's competitors as high prices will be profitable for these newcomers in the energy market.

77   Bloomberg: America hits Qatar and Russia at the core through gas. Op. cit. from: https://bit.ly/2nZB6T7

78   Clifford Crouch. The US wealth in liquefied natural gas threatens the world's energy. Op. cit. from: https://bit.ly/2H2GY6N

79   Ibid

80   David Sheppard and Henry Foy. The gas market... a Russian - American battle where Europe wins. Op. cit. from: https://bit.ly/2BojrNt

On the other hand, the Polish Foreign Minister, Witold Waszczykowski, for example, said his country is considering the feasibility of importing gas from the United States, stressing that his country has not yet taken a final decision on the purchase of US gas. Waszczykowski also confirmed his country's intention to purchase American gas if it offers competitive prices compared to those of other suppliers, such as Qatar and Russia. He noted that the US gas is extremely expensive, without specifying the price differential.[81]

What is more, in comparison to Russian or Qatari gas, US gas is "very expensive because it is a deep-rooted shale gas, and the processing and liquefaction of this gas and its transport by private vessels overseas is more expensive…Therefore, the US is currently only able to create better conditions for its companies to infiltrate the European markets, at the expense of Russian gas, through political lobbying and economic sanctions that violate International Law. It is also noteworthy that Qatar's competition is also enduring the repercussions of Arab sanctions on the country… Subsequently, it is possible to say that the US is trying to exercise economic despotism which also harms the interests of its closest long-term allies are contrary to the rules of world trade."[82] In addition, it is clear that gas transport through pipelines remains the least expensive means of transport, in addition to being the easiest and fastest means. This allows the supplier to ensure the smooth delivery of gas, while ensuring that there are no delays, compared to transporting in ship tankers, for example.

Gas Quantities

Although there is talk of huge stockpiles in the United States, Russian gas is still needed. According to the Bloomberg Agency,

---

81   Fred Geerley. 15/5/2018. The US threatens the "Nord Stream" with sanctions. Russia Today. (Retrieved on 25/11/2018) from: https://bit.ly/2INeEsP

82   Ibrahim Mohamed. 17/6/2017. American sanctions… a weapon for European energy market competition! DW. (Retrieved on: 23/6/2018) from: https://bit.ly/2G6ABhM

preparations are under way "in Europe to send the second shipment of Russian liquefied gas originating from one of its ports to the United States, which is trying to compete with Russia in the European gas market." Furthermore, the agency noted that PROVALYS, the tanker carrying Russian liquefied gas, will be leaving the French port of Dunkirk to the north east US, which faces a shortage of gas supplies during the peak demand period. This is the second largest Russian gas shipment to head to the US. In December 2017, the tanker, GASELYS left a British port headed to the US... The media interpreted that the US tendency to purchase Russian gas stems from its competitive price compared to the US current gas price in eastern US."[83] In addition, many estimates showed a decline in the US natural gas reserves in January 2018 in a way that exceeded analysts' expectations. The US Energy Information Administration data showed that US natural gas reserves are declining either monthly or yearly.[84] Therefore, it is possible to conclude that reserves are in decline. So how will the US be able to compete in a market which already suffers from a lack of materials or means of extraction in the first place?!

Transportation Security

One of the biggest problems surrounding this sector is the issue of energy security itself. Pipelines are considered to be somewhat safe, as security tensions, especially in straits and canals, may pose a major environmental threat to tankers.

Will Russia allow the US or its energy allies' tankers to compete with it at home and to cross its borders if the Nord Road is opened in the Arctic Ocean or the Strait of Hormuz, where Russia is deploying its military forces in or near these areas?

---

83   Fred Geerley. 28/1/2018. The US "forced" to purchase Russian gas. Russia Today. (Retrieved on: 17/3/2018) from: https://bit.ly/2EgS8Y1

84   American natural gas reserves in decline during the last week. 8/2/2018. Dostor Egyptian Newpaper. (Retrieved on: 15/5/2018) from: http://www.dostor.org/2052304

The European and Chinese Positions

The great difference between the positions of European countries and the United States on many international issues, such as the Iranian nuclear issue for example, may be a factor in their increasing disagreements. US sanctions against Russia, which most European countries see as damaging to their interests, are in Washington's full interest.[85]

For instance, the German objection to Washington's efforts to stop the Nord Stream – 2, is a clear position against Washington's energy policy. On top of this, American sanctions on Moscow also affected the European companies it deals with. Former German foreign minister, Sigmar Gabriel, accused Washington of seeking to achieve "its economic interests by intentionally lobbying and threatening European companies… threatening to impose these sanctions is a new negative transformation in the American - European relations."[86]

Consequently, here are some important questions. Will Washington be able to lobby its European partners to purchase its more expensive gas? In the event of submission, will the fear of European governments of their own people force the US to create a crisis to persuade them to abandon any non-American gas? Answering these questions is only a matter of time and depends on future developments. But it is difficult, at least in the meantime, for Europe to easily abandon Russian gas, as Alexander Medvedev, Deputy CEO of Gazprom said: "We are able to pump as much gas as Europe needs even though we are entering a new market in China. However, Europe has to decide now; they need to think rationally about who will cover increasing demands after 2025. Unfortunately, there is no energy

---

85 Fred Geerley. 25/5/2018. Russian Novatek signs a huge gas agreement with French Total. Russia Today. (Retrieved on: 3/7/2018) from: https://bit.ly/2sjyTVQ

86 Ibrahim Mohamed. American sanctions… a weapon for European energy market competition! Op. cit. from: https://bit.ly/2G6ABhM

dialogue between Russia and the European Union."[87]

For China, it is very difficult for them to rely on US gas, especially under the administration of President Donald Trump, who takes advantage of any opportunity to attack China. In addition, Russian-Chinese understandings are much deeper than they seem, as the two countries face the same common "enemy".

---

87   Moscow warns Europe against relying on US gas. Op. cit. from: https://bit.ly/2EiRA3Q

Strategic Water Canals

The Eurasia Canal: A Geopolitical Networking

After the introduction of the theory of Eurasia and work to find common Euro - Asian denominators, Russia started to witness fierce pressure. Therefore, Moscow had to find exits for the different crises it was facing, especially as the restrictions came mostly from Europe and the West to prevent Russia from being in Warm Water.

Given the importance of this region to global security in general and to Russian national security, especially as the Caucasus region poses a real threat, this canal becomes vital for Russia. Therefore, Moscow needs to consider implementing the canal in the most serious ways.

Historical Background

Armen Grigoryan, political planning adviser at the Armenian Foreign Ministry, said in a lecture at the UAE Media Center that the Euro - Asian project, which will link the Caspian Sea and the Black Sea, through a system of manmade canals, will revolutionize transport routes through Continents and will become a major hub for Russia's energy exports in Central Asia. According to Grigoryan, the project was "was proposed by the former President of Kazakhstan, Nursultan Nazarbayev, at the 11th World Economic Forum, held on 10 June 2007 in St. Petersburg, as an alternative to the Volga - Don canal already in southwestern Russia and which connects the Caspian and Black Seas along 151-km."[1]

---

1   A Caspian - Black Sea canal via manmade canal system will revolutionize goods transportation. 6/11/2007. Al-Watan Voice. (Retrieved on: 8/11/2018) from: https://bit.ly/2GGrkRb

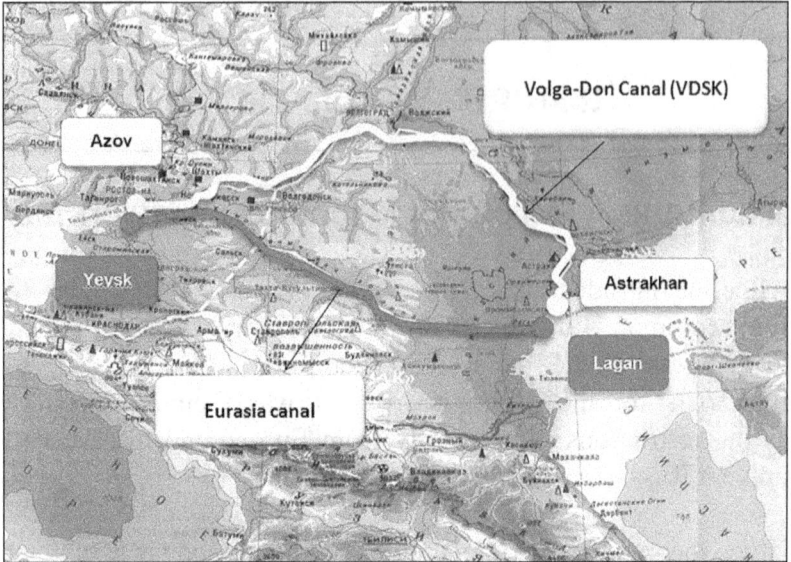

The Eurasia Canal primary plan.

In this regard, the Kazakh president said that the canal is the axis of economic transit without political considerations, he pointed out that his proposal is to build a new river canal from the Black Sea through the Sea of Azov to connect to the Volga - Don canal, which was constructed during Stalin's reign, and then the Volga River, which flows into the Caspian Sea.[2] This canal was built by Stalin for use in shipping transport operations; however, the problem is that navigation may be interrupted as snow accumulates during several months of the year. The canal is located completely in Russian territory and is long because it does not go in a straight line but follows the river Volga's curves and zigzags[3] to reach Astrakhan on the Caspian Sea.

Due to the importance of the project, data suggests that The Eurasian Development Bank earmarked $2.7 million for a

---

2   Kazakh President suggests a new Caspian - Black Sea canal. 11/6/2007. Al-Rai. (Retrieved on: 25/7/2018) from: https://bit.ly/2GZY5GU

3   Mohamed Khalifah. 26/6/2007. A canal links the Caspian Sea to the Black Sea. Al-Watan Voice. (Retrieved on: 17/8/2018) from: https://bit.ly/2uzIaMR

feasibility study of the Eurasia canal and Volga – Don 2 shipway – another possible yet more costly and lengthy option" Furthermore, Kalmyk authorities in Russia "have already held negotiations with India and China on engineering works and hydro-construction. Beijing, in turn, has expressed its desire to fund the construction of the Eurasia canal. The latter may have an international status and is expected to be much cheaper and faster, generating millions of dollars in transit fees for Kazakhstan and Russia. To put this in perspective, if the 'Western Europe – Western China' road connecting China, Russia, and Kazakhstan obtains a 5% transit share of current Europe - Asia sea cargo, the transit countries could receive around $3 billion in transit fees annually."[4]

The Canal's Route and Cost

Some modifications have been made to this project's route to be replaced by the Yeysk[5] – Lagan[6] corridor within the Manych sea canal which will extend to a distance of about 650 - 700 km (or a little bit further) and 29-km will pass through Stavropol in Russia.[7]

The Yeysk – Manych – Lagan canal was completed on-time, marking the first step in a comprehensive series of internal projects to be completed within the Russian Federation during the year. The canal is intended to provide a shorter route for shipping than the existing Volga - Don canal system of waterways.

As for the project's parameters, information determines that "the depth throughout the system is targeted at 6.5m, with a width of 110m." So, "the Manych Sea Canal will need to be considerably expanded to allow for larger ships. The eastern course of the

---

4   Roman Muzalevsky. 1/10/2010. The Kazakh - Russian "Eurasia" Canal: The Geopolitics of Water, Transport, and Trade. Eurasia Daily Monitor. Vol: 7. Issue No.: 177. (Retrieved on: 10/5/2018) from: https://bit.ly/2I8h8lW

5   The Town of Yeysk in the Russian "Krasnodar Krai" area on the Azov Sea.

6   The village of Lagan at the "Lagansky" District on the Caspian Sea

7   A Caspian - Black Sea canal via manmade canal system will revolutionize goods transportation. Op. cit. from: https://bit.ly/2GGrkRb

(Kuma River) will also see large construction to connect the Caspian Sea to the Black Sea, whilst also cutting down the number of mid-rise locks needed on the canal." Yet, to keep water levels sufficiently high, it is necessary to install water locks. "It is required that the western slope will need three mid-rise locks, with the eastern slope needing four mid-rise locks, this cuts the number of locks needed to transit from the Black Sea to the Caspian Sea in half, cutting the transit time by a large amount."

With respect to financial cost, some reports indicate "the total of $1.7 billion has been appropriated by the State Duma for the construction of locks, along with an additional $6 billion for the expansion of the existing Manych Ship Canal, the Kuma River and the pipeline supplying the canal with water from the mouth of Volga. If all goes as planned, the project is expected to take six and a half years, opening June 2024."[8]

Project's Characteristics

This project has great importance and abundant advantages, the most prominent of which lies in:

Environmentally Speaking

- High water levels in the canal will help irrigate surrounding agricultural lands, which will allow for the expansion of agricultural land and increase crops.

- The project may also help fishery workers as it will allow the establishment of fish farms on the banks of the canal.

- Hydroelectric power plants could be constructed at the base

8   Natalia V. Poklonskaya. 27/6/2017. The Eurasian Canal, Unleashing the Caspian Tiger! Reddit. (Retrieved on: 10/5/2018) from: https://bit.ly/2G4I0NQ Also: A Caspian - Black Sea manmade canal system will revolutionize goods transportation. Op. cit. from: https://bit.ly/2GGrkRb

The North-South Transport Corridor which links India to its Eurasian surrounding through Iran.

of canal facilities. These plants could significantly increase the operating benefits of wind power plants planned to be constructed in the Republic of Kalmykia and the Stavropol region. Canal facilities could include water reservoirs up-slope of the canal for a hydroelectric power scheme that operates at peak times or when there is no wind to operate the water locks. This will activate the water locks as each lock needs about 60 Megawatts of electricity[9], all this using clean energy.

Economically Speaking

• Reducing time and distance between Central Asia and Europe from the Black Sea portal and the Baltic Sea, especially after the completion of the so-called North - South Corridor[10] which starts from India, via Iran, to the Russian port of St. Petersburg on the waters of the Baltic Sea.

---

9   Manych Ship Canal. No Date. Wikipedia. (retrieved on: 10/5/2018) from: https://bit.ly/2wxyd3x

10   Iran and Russia's Giant corridor en route to compete with the Suez Canal. 10/8/2016. Noon Post. (Retrieved on: 7/10/2018) from: https://bit.ly/2IlsXBg

- On April 9th 2016, the Iranian Ambassador to Russia, Mehdi Sanaei, confirmed that Moscow and Tehran conducted talks on constructing a navigational canal linking the Caspian Sea to the Persian Gulf. This was also confirmed by Russian Foreign Minister, Sergei Lavrov, on April 7th of the same year when he said that Russia, Iran, and Azerbaijan all agreed to intensify the talks pertaining to the construction of the 7,200-km North - South transport corridor, part of which will pass along the western coast of the Caspian Sea from Russia to Iran via Azerbaijan.[11] The corridor, which links the Russian cities of St. Petersburg and India's Mumbai, is expected to reduce shipping times of vessels coming from India to Central Asia and Russia from 40 to 14 days.[12]

The project is based on a map drawn up in 2000[13] by Iran, India, and Russia, but the sanctions imposed on Tehran and Moscow have prevented the construction of this corridor, which consists of sea and land lines and railways.[14] The idea was first tested by transporting goods from India to the Azerbaijani capital of Baku and Astrakhan through the port of Bandar Abbas in Iran in 2014.[15]

- If this project is completed along with the Eurasian canal, they will link the Five Seas[16] (Caspian, Black, Mediterranean, Red

---

11 Moscow - Tehran - Baku: An agreement on a land corridor covering the coast of Caspian Sea. 8/4/2016. Al-Akhbar Lebanese Newspaper. (Retrieved on: 7/11/2017) from: https://al-akhbar.com/World/7199

12 Moscow and Tehran discuss building a sailing canal linking the Caspian Sea to the Persian Gulf. 9/4/2016. Russia Today. (Retrieved on: 18/9/2018) from: https://bit.ly/2pv11mb

13 Abdel Jalil Zeid. 6/6/2008. After oil and gas pipelines... railways draw the conflict lines on the Caucasus. Al-Riyadh Newspaper. (Retrieved on: 5/9/2018) from: http://www.alriyadh.com/348512

14 Iran opens a railway accelerating trade with Russia. 5/10/2014. Sputnik. (Retrieved on: 14/6/2018) from: https://bit.ly/2rByvR7

15 Iran and Russia's Giant corridor en route to compete with the Suez Canal. Op. cit. from: https://bit.ly/2IlsXBg

16 In this regard, see: Alwan N. Amin Eddine. Sino – German Relations 1990 – 2015: In Light of Economic Strategies and Policies. Isticharia. Beirut –

and Gulf Seas), a geopolitical proposal suggested by Syrian President, Bashar al-Assad. This would allow for the opening of waterways through all seas and linking them tightly and coherently at all levels[17], especially with the wealth of huge natural resources and a tremendous human strength of more than 200 million people.[18]

- This project will allow large freighters to cross whereas the ships that cross the Volga - Don are small and have a relatively small load. These freighters will be able to "carry 45 million tons of cargo per year and accommodate large fleets."[19]

- Russia will become a transit country within the Black – Azov – Caspian Sea triangle, thus increasing Russian exports.[20]

- Russia will be also able to charge transit fees from crossing freights, which will generate huge annual financial returns.[21]

- Job opportunities will be created within vital projects conducted on the canal banks, such as resorts or specialized centers to serve ships passing by.

- The project, in this respect, is not in the interest of Russia alone, but many countries may benefit from it significantly. For example, Kazakhstan considers the project to be of major

Lebanon. 1st Edition. P: 300.

17   The Five Seas that will rule the world theory. 13/10/2017. Al-Alam News. (Retrieved on: 7/9/2018) from: https://bit.ly/2IbZGsN

18   Abdullah Bin Amarah. 27/1/2014. Networking the Five Seas Theory... as a Levant alternative. Al-Akhbar Lebanese Newspaper. (Retrieved on: 15/5/2018) from: https://www.al-akhbar.com/Opinion/25963

19   A Caspian - Black Sea canal via manmade canal system will revolutionize goods transportation. Op. cit. from: https://bit.ly/2GGrkRb

20   A canal linking the Caspian and the Black sea and will revolutionize goods transportation. 6/11/2007. Al-Ittihad Newspaper. (Retrieved on: 15/6/2017) from: https://bit.ly/2E9apS0

21   Roman Muzalevsky. The Kazakh - Russian "Eurasia" Canal: The Geopolitics of Water, Transport, and Trade. Op. cit. from: https://bit.ly/2I8h8lW

importance because it will allow it to access global markets throughout the year.[22]

Energy Speaking

- Central Asia is a reservoir for huge energy natural resources. The Caspian Sea[23] alone is very important for its huge oil and gas reserves existing in the Sea and the countries that surround it. Data suggests that these reserves are the second in the world after those of the GCC countries.[24]

- Completing this project will increase Russian oil exports with yearly revenues going from $30 to $40 billion.[25]

- This project will reduce distances and time with the largest oil carriers in the world crossing the canal.[26]

- The Russian network for water transportation will be integrated into international transportation frameworks related to the Caspian Sea, the Black Sea, and the Mediterranean.[27]

---

22   A Caspian - Black Sea canal via manmade canal system will revolutionize goods transportation. Op. cit. from: https://bit.ly/2GGrkRb

23   Due to the importance of this closed sea, the riparian countries of the Caspian Sea held a historic summit in the Kazakh city of Aktau and signed a very important agreement regarding economic, political and security aspects. In this regards, see: Yara Enbeaa. 14/8/2018. The Caspian Sea... a "sovereign property of bordering states". Sita Institute. (Retrieved on: 28/10/2018) from: https://sitainstitute.com/?p=3271
Also see: Amin Eddine: "Caspian Agreement" is historical in hinge time. 20/8/2018. Sita Institute. (Retrieved on: 28/10/2018) from: https://sitainstitute.com/?p=3305

24   Mohamed Khalifah. 26/6/2007. A canal links the Caspian Sea to the Black Sea. Al-Watan Voice. (Retrieved on: 15/8/2018) from: https://bit.ly/2uzIaMR

25   A Caspian - Black Sea canal via manmade canal system will revolutionize goods transportation. Op. cit. from: https://bit.ly/2GGrkRb

26   Mohamed Khalifah. A canal links the Caspian Sea to the Black Sea. Op. cit. from: https://bit.ly/2uzIaMR

27   A Caspian - Black Sea canal via manmade canal system will revolutionize goods transportation. Op. cit. from: https://bit.ly/2GGrkRb

Strategically Speaking

- The project is in conformity with President Vladimir Putin's proposal in 2007 "for the expansion of inland water-ways within the country, stating that a canal connecting the two seas will not only provide the Caspian bordering countries with access to the Black and Mediterranean Seas, (the seven seas), but qualitatively change their geopolitical position and allow them to become the maritime powers. The project is expected to contribute to the development of Russia's southern regions and the Caucasus."[28]

- The entire canal will be under Russian control, making it a sovereign canal in the first place and protected by a vital area of land on the south, which is some 340-km from the border with Georgia.

- The canal will allow for freedom of movement of the Caspian Sea and Black Sea military fleets in both directions, as this canal will not only allow the passage of river vessels, but many Russian naval vessels, including warships and even nuclear submarines.[29]

Obstacles and Challenges

Despite all the advantages, the project faces many challenges, mainly:

Environmental Factors

- Drilling the canal will increase the internal water salinity, undermining water life and endangering its banks.

---

28 Roman Muzalevsky. The Kazakh - Russian "Eurasia" Canal: The Geopolitics of Water, Transport, and Trade. Op. cit. from: https://bit.ly/2I8h8lW

29 Natalia V. Poklonskaya. The Eurasian Canal, Unleashing the Caspian Tiger! Op. cit. from: https://bit.ly/2G4I0NQ

- Increasing pollution rates caused by shipping especially if they do not comply with environmental guidelines.

- Natural conditions may affect the canal such as snow accumulation which may prevent ship access at certain times of the year, in addition to problems related to filling the canal with water especially from the southern Russian borders because of water scarcity.[30]

- The project's implementation will not only clash with the interests of countries in the Caspian basin, but also of those in the Black Sea region where there are parties interested and active, especially in terms of environmental issues. These are a real impediment to the project, especially for countries which may be affected by damage to the environment[31], such as Iran which depends on this sea to produce its caviar.

Logistical Factors

- The existence of several water locks will delay transportation operations, especially since they will require periodical maintenance.

- Some areas are not ready yet for this project as they need special rehabilitation to meet the project's sheer volume. For example, the absence of technical facilities in the port of Kalmikatan – Lagan on the Caspian coast makes the project impossible to achieve.[32]

Political Factors

- The Caucasus region, Georgia and Armenia, in particular, in addition to Ukraine, are experiencing many tensions that

---

30 A Caspian - Black Sea canal via manmade canal system will revolutionize goods transportation. Op. cit. from: https://bit.ly/2GGrkRb

31 Ibid.

32 Ibidem.

could significantly harm Russia if triggered, thus hindering the canal's ability to perform its commercial role.

- Drilling and operating the canal will make Russia's role pivotal in the area, which raises concerns in many neighboring countries, especially the European ones.

- European countries fear the vital role that Moscow might possibly play after linking the continent with gas. This comes at a time when fears of Russian expansion are rising on the continent.[33]

- The United States will never stand still in the face of this Russian competitive achievement, especially following the expansion policy adopted through NATO in the East and the attempts that have been made to lure Russia into armed tensions to limit its progress. Many observers believe that Washington is pursuing a hostile policy against Russia aimed at dominating it and preventing it from maintaining its independence and strength.[34]

---

33   Ibidem.

34   Mohamed Khalifah. A canal links the Caspian Sea to the Black Sea. Op. cit. from: https://bit.ly/2uzIaMR

The Kanal Istanbul: An Opening to the Saros Canal?

The Montreux convention, signed in 1936, which amended the provisions of the 1923 Lausanne convention regarding the Straits, remains a concern, if not a problem, on a strategic level for Turkey. The Convention puts the Dardanelles and Bosphorus straits under specific provisions which impede Ankara's independent mobility.

In this regard, Turkey's Minister of Transport, Communications and Maritime Navigation, Ahmet Arslan, referred to the so-called Kanal Istanbul in determining the canal's route. Arslan noted that "the fourth alternative route has been determined and will cross the Küçükçekmece – Sazlıdere - Durusu corridor." Minister Arslan also pointed out that the length of the canal will be about 45-km[35], while the length of the Bosphorus is about 30-km, with a width of 150m.[36] According to Turkish statistics, "137 cargo ships and 27 tankers carrying 150 million tons of commercial cargo will cross the canal."[37]

While the merits of the project are still being studied carefully, some modifications will be required. According to some press reports, there has been a change in the canal project to reduce its cost by 30 billion Turkish liras ($6.5 billion) by reducing the canal's width from 400 to 275 meters. The drilling volume is also expected to decrease from 1.7 billion to 800 million cubic meters, making bridge constructions less costly which will allow for the construction of 7 instead of 6 bridges as per the most recent plan. The project will be supervised through the Office of the Presidency of the Kanal Istanbul project to

35 Nadejda Anyutina. 15/1/2018. Turkey reveals the "Kanal Istanbul" route. Russia Today. (Retrieved on: 25/3/2018) from: https://bit.ly/2E4UhoO

36 Khaleel Mabruk. 14/10/2017. Istanbul water canal compensates for Turkey's "Montreux" losses. Al-Jazeera. (Retrieved on: 14/6/2018) from: https://bit.ly/2FEaBtC

37 Nadejda Anyutina. Turkey reveals the "Kanal Istanbul" route. Op. cit. from: https://bit.ly/2E4UhoO

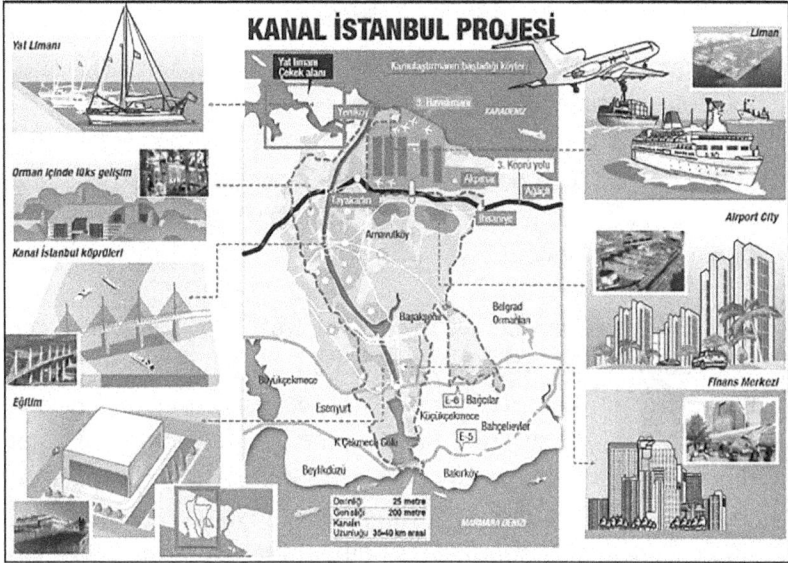

Istanbul water canal

be created in cooperation with the Presidency of the Turkish General Administration of Housing (TOKİ), Emlak Konut, and the Greater Istanbul Municipality.[38] From this perspective, this canal is important for Turkey on many levels, most notably:

Economic Importance

- It creates new vital zones capable of attracting populations since it is considered one of the most active cargo ship routes.[39] However, this will require removing random buildings constructed along the route.[40]

- The Turkish Ministry of Transportation will be launching tenders to build artificial islands, in addition to those which

---

38   New amendments to the sea Canal Istanbul project. 6/7/2018. Turk Press. (Retrieved on: 19/10/2018) from: http://www.turkpress.co/node/50913

39   Nadejda Anyutina. Turkey reveals the "Kanal Istanbul" route. Op. Cit. from: https://bit.ly/2E4UhoO

40   Istanbul Canal... The biggest project in Turkey's history. 20/1/2018. Al-Jazeera. (Retrieved on: 15/10/2018) from: https://bit.ly/2DPHxmK

will be constructed inside the Marmara Sea. The plan is to fill coal mines with the debris from excavations, in addition to the construction of recreation areas.[41]

• A new airport will be built in the region, which is expected to receive its first flights in late February 2018. It was officially opened in October 29th 2018.[42]

• The pollution caused by the heavy traffic of vessels in the Bosphorus Strait will be mitigated, in addition to minimizing the damage caused by vessels transporting hazardous materials.[43] On the other hand, some specialists believe that the opening of the canal "will have a significant impact on the complex structure of Turkish water systems." The water bodies around Istanbul, especially the Mediterranean Sea, which is part of the Marmara Sea and the Black Sea, differ in their saline composition and nutritive contents as they differ thousands of years in age. This difference makes it impossible to mix and harmonize the waters from the two seas, such as the impossibility of mixing oil and water."[44]

• Turkey will be fully free to impose fees on crossing ships. Ankara is still struggling with the transit and crossing tariffs imposed in the Turkish straits using the gold franc as a currency. In 1982, Turkey "stabilized the exchange rate of the gold franc, but has been discussing for some time the possibility of returning to the use of the gold franc in the determination of fees from transit vessels from the straits,

41 Ibid.

42 Nadejda Anyutina. Turkey reveals the "Kanal Istanbul" route. Op. cit. from: https://bit.ly/2E4UhoO
    Also see: Amid the festive atmosphere... Erdoğan opens the largest airport in the world today. 29/10/2018. Al-Jazeera. (Retrieved on: 25/11/2018) from: https://bit.ly/2EMDisI

43 Istanbul Canal... The biggest project in Turkey's history. Op. cit. from: https://bit.ly/2DPHxmK)

44 Khaleel Mabruk. Istanbul water canal compensates for Turkey's "Montreux" losses. Op. cit. from: https://bit.ly/2FEaBtC

which will significantly increase the financial burden on Russian ships (specifically)." From here, some Turkish economists believe that this re-pricing process, compared to the 2013 fee, will generate about $3 billion more in Turkey.[45]

- The canal will generate "substantial financial gains for Turkey to compensate for the funds it has been deprived of for 31 years following the Montreux convention." According to official Turkish reports the canal will generate "about $8 billion year", and "within 2 years the profits from the new canal will cover the cost of the $15 billion project, and will transform the historic Bosphorus into a secondary maritime trade line compared to the new canal that will attract ships and tankers."[46]

- The inauguration of the Kanal Istanbul, like the new Suez Canal, on both Bosphorus (Kanal Istanbul) lines will "motivate ships to avoid waiting the queues they have to go through in the Bosphorus, which will benefit Turkey financially."[47]

Political Importance

- Turkish president, Recep Tayyip Erdoğan, said that his country will take all necessary steps to achieve the Kanal Istanbul. He noted that "the Kanal will be a new leading worldwide trademark." Erdoğan confirmed how important this project is as Turkey "will acquire a position that exceeds the Suez and the Panama canals... we will make our first step the soonest possible."[48]

---

45   Ismail Jamal. 7/12/2015. Russian warships provoke Turkey in the Strait, Is Ankara entitled to the right to close the "Dardanelles" and "Bosporus" in the face of Putin's warships? Al-Quds Al-Arabai (Retrieved on: 18/10/2018) from: https://bit.ly/2DVIeb4

46   Khaleel Mabruk. Istanbul water canal compensates for Turkey's "Montreux" losses. Op. cit. from: https://bit.ly/2FEaBtC

47   Mahmud Samir Rantisi. 17/1/2018. The Kanal Istanbul water project... a new Bosporus which will increase Turkey's influence. Noon Post. (Retrieved on: 6/11/2018) from: https://bit.ly/2BPGdtS

48   Samir Hosni. 7/10/2017. Erdoğan is rambling: Kanal Istanbul will exceed Suez

- The canal is one of the giant projects that accompanied the Vision 2023, adopted by Turkey as a mid-term development plan through which it wants to be amongst the ten most influential countries in the world by the 100th anniversary of the founding of the modern Turkish Republic.[49]

- The Turkish president's achievements gained him large popular support as he won the presidential elections held in June 2018, instead of 2019 as previously planned[50], and the Turkish people voted for him to have additional presidential powers. In addition, the president is attempting to gain even more powers to allow him to determine his country's foreign policy on economic grounds in the future.

Strategic Importance

- "This project is not only important for Turkey but also for regional and international geography," said many Turkish strategists. "It will not be a route for local transport but a route to trade, energy, economy, transport and technology in the region."[51]

- This will allow for exemption from certain provisions of the Montreux convention, in particular paragraphs specifying the total tonnage of the sea vessels coming from countries outside the Black Sea basin and other countries, and the period in which the ships should leave the Strait (estimated at 21 days as the duration of residence in the Black Sea)[52],

canal in importance. Youm 7. (Retrieved on: 29/10/2018) from: https://bit.ly/2DXCcK6

49   Khaleel Mabruk. Istanbul water canal compensates for Turkey's "Montreux" losses. Op. cit. from: https://bit.ly/2FEaBtC

50   Yara Enbeaa. 25/6/2018. Turkish "presidential" elections: Strategic transformations. Sita Institute. (Retrieved on: 7/10/2018) from: https://sitainstitute.com/?p=2955

51   Mahmud Samir Rantisi. The Kanal Istanbul water project... a New Bosporus which will increase Turkey's influence. Op. cit. from: https://bit.ly/2BPGdtS

52   The Montreux Convention. 8/12/2015. Al-Jazeera. (Retrieved on: 10/10/2018)

and the number of warships that must be in the strait at the same time (only nine ships).[53] Hence, ships that cross into the Black Sea using this canal will not be subject to the terms and conditions of the said agreement, which will place international responsibility on Turkey.

- Turkey can prevent ships, even commercial ones and not only warships, from crossing in the event of any future amendments to the Montreux Convention. Some Russian media previously stated that the Turkish authorities sought to impede their ships' access through the Bosporus.[54] From an objective perspective, an event of this kind will have great repercussions, especially on Russia as the Strait is its only passage to Warm Waters and Russia will never accept this kind of situation. But no one can predict the future and the plans of countries. Russia, for example, has agreed with Tehran to build a canal linking the Bandar Abbas region of Iran to the Caspian Sea, allowing Russian ships there to reach the Gulf region in a significant and effective manner. Thus, thinking about such a project is an important strategic vision that Russia and Iran both value.

- The canal will be under the rule of Turkish domestic law, therefore it can put any conditions it deems appropriate. A number of experts in international law have pointed out that the Montreux agreement would not have anything to do with the Kanal Istanbul in principle, and that "its legal assessment process would be different from the natural straits such as the Bosphorus. Military speaking, the project will certainly have a significant role in the military budgets."[55]

---

from: https://bit.ly/2nwwF2N

53 Ismail Jamal. Russian warships provoke Turkey in the Strait, Is Ankara entitled to the right to close the "Dardanelles" and "Bosporus" in the face of Putin's warships? Op. cit. from: https://bit.ly/2DVleb4

54 Ibid

55 Mahmud Samir Rantisi. The Kanal Istanbul water project... a new Bosporus which will increase Turkey's influence. Op. cit from: https://bit.ly/2BPGdtS

Will This Canal Be a Prelude For Saros?

Here a big question arises: Is the Kanal Istanbul a prelude for the Saros Gulf Canal? It is plausible to say that this is very likely to happen for many reasons, namely:

- A quick look at Google Maps reveals the approximate distance between the Gulf of Saros and Marmara Sea, with an average distance of about 4.5-km, making the idea feasible, especially since the Dardanelles Strait reaches about 61-km in length.

- The width of the Dardanelles varies between 1.2-km and 6-km. Therefore, building the Saros Canal could be beneficial especially for departing ships, making regular crossings (back and forth) easier.

- This canal, if built, will be closer to Europe. Ships coming from the west side of the Mediterranean currently have to circumvent several kilometers before entering the straits, so there will be a saving of time and distance.

- The nature of the waters in the area is the same as both waters are Mediterranean.

- Turkey will be able to gain substantial profits out of the canal. The drilling cost will not be the same as that of Kanal Istanbul. If Turkey needs two years to recover the cost of the Istanbul, the recovery period will be much less for this one.

- The canal will also fall under Turkish Sovereign Laws.

- Strategically speaking, Turkey will be able to avoid the provisions of the Montreux convention and allow ships access the canal as it deems appropriate. In this regard, it may be a real threat to some of the Black Sea countries, namely Russia, since Turkey is a NATO member and has an army of 600,000 soldiers. NATO ships would be able to freely cross in and out

Strategic Water Canals

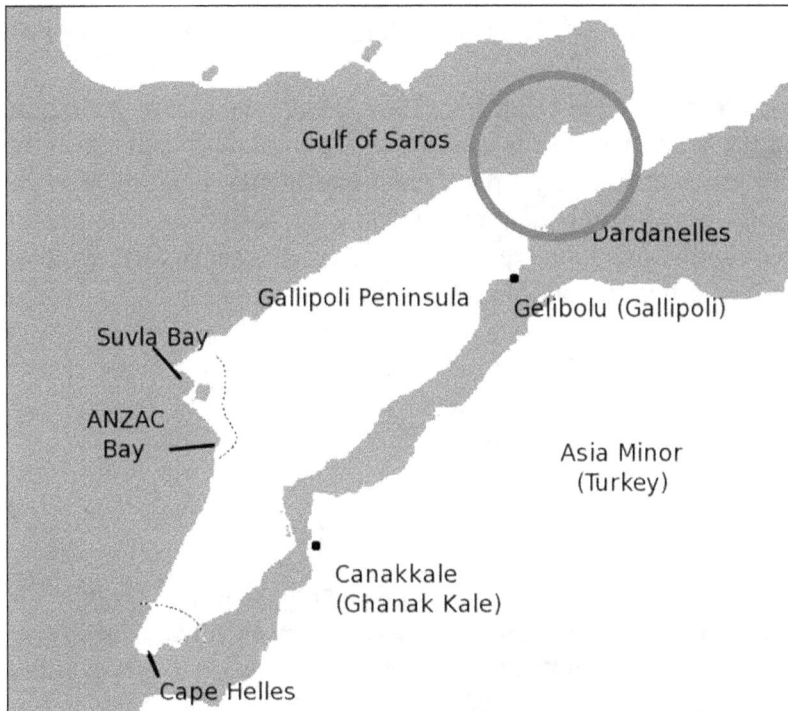

Saros Canal suggested route.

of the sea, in a way that will surely annoy Moscow.

For objectivity, such a project is subject to geological studies, water depth, and other details.

Saudi Water Canals Justification and Purpose

Saudi Arabia seeks to increase its influence and role in the region in the framework of its so-called Vision 2030. It relies heavily on the vision as a major project to jumpstart its economy. Riyadh is also a self-proclaimed regional Islamic power which wants to play a vital role in the region given the high security threats that, in its opinion, are pushing it to play a leading role.

Hence, the Kingdom's policy was to find strategic water canals that would allow retaining real control over an area it considered a matter of national security.

Salman Water Canal

The head of AL-Qarn AL-Arabi Research & Studies Center, Dr. Saad Bin Omar, revealed that the KSA seeks to create the largest sea canal project in the region, enabling navigators to access the region away from the Strait of Hormuz.[56]

The study was prepared in a Riyadh based center for studies and is based on the development of a major canal route and two reserve routes. The main route starts at Saudi Arabia's part of the Gulf, specifically at Khawr al Udayd (near southern Qatar) and heads towards the Arabian Sea through the Rub' al Khali desert. It is 950-km long, 630-km of which are in the KSA and 320-km in the Yemeni territory, and it is 150m wide and 25m deep.[57] There are two routes at the northern part of the canal: the first is adjacent to Qatar's western border (a standby route), and the second at the southern borders. The same goes for the canal's end where the main route goes through Yemen and the standby route is in Oman.

---

56   The Salman Canal: from the Gulf to the Arabian Sea. 28/10/2015. National Kuwait. (Retrieved on: 27/10/2018) from: https://bit.ly/2KtKybN

57   The "Salman Canal"... what is the Saudi's purpose for the project? 16/9/2015. Syria Now News. (Retrieved on: 17/11/2008) from: https://bit.ly/2HJp1Kt

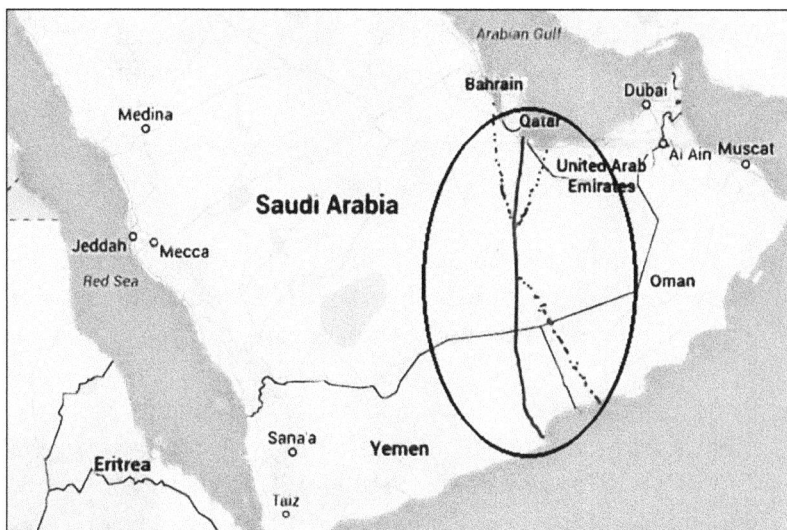

Planned route of the Salman Water Canal

Many analysts say that the KSA is in an appropriate position to take executive measures for the project start. Many national companies are about to complete incumbent projects and have huge supplies and a trained manpower able to conduct drilling and construction. The estimated timetable for the project's completion is five years[58] at a cost of $80 billion.[59]

Economic value

- Once the project is completed, "a new life for the Rub' al Khali desert will see the development of hotels and tourist resorts built on the canal's banks." [60]

- The Head of AL Qarn Center, Dr. Bin Omar, said that "the

---

58   Abdul Rahmann Abu Al Futuh. 14/9/2015. The "Salman Canal" what is the Saudi purpose behind this water crossing project? Sasa Post. (Retrieved on: 25/10/2018) from: https://bit.ly/2KoA0uu

59   The "Salman Canal"… what is the Saudi's purpose for the project? Op. cit. from: https://bit.ly/2HJp1Kt

60   Abdul Rahmann Abu Al Futuh. The "Salman Canal" what is the Saudi purpose behind this water crossing project? Op. cit. from: https://bit.ly/2KoA0uu

Canal will add 1200-km of clean and beautiful coasts (on the canal's shorelines) at the Saudi Empty Quarter region."[61]

- Until completion, the project will help create about a million new job opportunities.[62]

- The Kingdom will be self-sufficient in terms of fisheries which will be built on both sides of the canal along with connected lakes created for this purpose.[63]

- Projects related to energy and water desalination will be built in addition to residential cities that exceed those of the TAPLINE (Trans - Arabian Pipeline) in the northern side of the Kingdom.[64]

- Many sea canals will be built within the Kingdom with each canal ending in one lake. On the other hand, on each lake a nuclear power plant will be established in Rub' al Khali away from the main cities. Power will be produced at no less than 50 Gigawatts. According to engineer Esmat Al-Hakeem's project study, the Kingdom will turn into a leading and exporting power in peaceful nuclear projects, industries, agricultural fields, animal farms, fisheries, and new energy facilities.[65]

- It will benefit from the housing, agriculture and irrigation projects in the Empty Quarter through the establishment

---

61   Fahd al-Otaibi Bin Omar details. 2/9/2015. The "Salman Canal": It will bring the Empty Quarter back to life. Sabq Online Newspaper. (Retrieved on: 19/10/2018) from: https://bit.ly/2rarnfo

62   The Hormuz Alternative "Salman Canal" is revealed and will cross the Empty Quarter to Yemini shores, "Details". 9/9/2015. Al-Yemni Al-Jadeed. (Retrieved on: 9/11/2018) from: https://bit.ly/2HI8bQ4

63   Abdul Rahmann Abu Al Futuh. The "Salman Canal" what is the Saudi purpose behind this water crossing project? Op. cit. from: https://bit.ly/2KoA0uu

64   Ibid.

65   Saudi Arabia... Revealing the artificial Salman Canal details. 20/4/2016. Alkhaleej Online. (Retrieved on: 11/11/2018) from: https://bit.ly/2w2xGX9

of modern cities at the branches of these marine canals to accommodate the workers in the upcoming projects, including generation stations, industrial projects, agriculture, livestock and irrigation.[66]

- The KSA will drill 20 tunnels for cars and pedestrians and it plans three residential, and two industrial cities.[67]

- The Kingdom will be able to transport its oil through the canal.[68] This is especially important since huge amounts of oil are located in the Northern part of the country.

- Ships crossing through the canal to the Arabian Sea will be able to halve the distance crossed through the Strait of Hormuz.[69]

- On the Yemeni side, the Canal will add 650-km of shorelines (on both sides), providing many job opportunities and investments for the country.

- Specialized Sea projects will provide better logistic services for crossing ships.[70]

- The countries where the Canal passes will be able to collect transit tariffs from crossing carriers, providing an additional income for their treasuries.

---

66   Ibid.

67   Maps: Salman competes with Suez and threatens Jebel Ali. No Date. Elshaab Al-Jadeed, (Retrieved on: 17/11/2018) from: https://bit.ly/2rdielo
     Also see: Mohamed Abdul Jawad. 8/9/2015. Maps… "King Salman Canal", a new logistic pole to link the Gulf to the Arabian Sea at a cost of $80 Billion. Elbalad. (Retrieved on: 25/10/2018) from: https://bit.ly/2KsCEiP

68   "Salman Canal"… to "end" the role of Hormuz Strait! 21/04/2016. Lebanon Debate. (Retrieved on: 13/11/2018) from: https://bit.ly/2jlCVbi

69   The Hormuz Alternative "Salman Canal" is revealed and will cross the Empty Quarter to Yemini shores, "Details". Op. cit. from: https://bit.ly/2HI8bQ4

70   Maps: Salman competes with Suez and threatens Jebel Ali. Op. cit. from: https://bit.ly/2rdielo

- Some call this project KSA's Second renaissance[71] because of its strategic importance.

Logistic Obstacles and Environmental Risks

Despite the above benefits, there are obstacles and caveats that impede the construction of such a canal, mainly:

- The practical benefit of the project "does not match its high cost which may even be considered a waste of public money, especially given the existence of the Strait of Hormuz."[72]

- Some specialists consider there are some logistical obstacles including the altitude of the canal especially in the Yemeni (or Omani) part. The highest altitude in Saudi Arabia is 300m above sea level, while some part of Yemen (or Oman) is as high as 700m above sea level.[73]

- The environmental risks are much greater than the project's economic importance especially if groundwater is taken into consideration. Many environmental reports say that by 2050, due to ice melting, "sea levels will rise by one meter. [They] confirm that fresh groundwater will be salinized. As a result, many regions of the world will suffer major problems."[74] Therefore, experts see that "groundwater is more important than any other project. Water is irreplaceable. The canal's project is pure suicide. The groundwater in the Empty Quarter is a strategic reserve that should be preserved for future generations."[75]

---

71   "Salman Canal"... to "end" the role of Hormuz Strait! Op. cit. from: https://bit.ly/2jlCVbi

72   The "Salman Canal"... what is the Saudi's purpose for the project? Op. cit. from: https://bit.ly/2HJp1Kt

73   Fahd al-Otaibi Bin Omar details. The "Salman Canal": It will bring the Empty Quarter back to life. Op. cit. from: https://bit.ly/2rarnfo Also see The "Salman Canal"... what is the Saudi's purpose for the project? Op. cit. from: https://bit.ly/2HJp1Kt

74   Dr. Mohamed Hamed Al-Ghamdy. 14/9/2015. The Salman Canal, looking for absurdity and illusion. Al-Youm. (Retrieved on: 19/11/2018) from: https://bit.ly/2rd5QT3

75   Ibid.

Security Justifications

Given the above obstacles, it is possible to discuss the reasons behind the Kingdom's plans to establish the canal project. The most prominent reasons are as follows:

- Energy security is one of Riyadh's main concerns especially since petroleum is the country's financial backbone.

- Through this project, the KSA would be attempting to circumvent Iran's influence on the Strait of Hormuz and deprive it of its strategic option to close the strait off to ships in the event of any aggressions by superpowers or wars occurring in the region.[76] This was revealed by Dr. Bin Omar who noted that the canal "will provide the Arab countries such as Qatar, the UAE and Kuwait with a route for oil transportation away from the Strait of Hormuz"[77], meaning away from any threat.

Meanwhile, analysts remark that this project is unfeasible due to the following:

- If the main purpose was to preserve energy security, it is possible to reach agreement with Muscat to extend oil transportation pipelines through its territory to the Arabian Sea, therefore saving huge amounts of money that would be spent on the canal.

- It will be difficult to reach a consensus in the Gulf to achieve such a project as it will pass through some of the GCC countries, and therefore there needs to be "a common political will from all of the GCC countries, and agreement on

---

76   The "Salman Canal"... what is the Saudi's purpose for the project? Op. cit. from: https://bit.ly/2HJp1Kt
     Also see The "Salman Canal"... what is the Saudi's purpose for the project? 15/9/2015. Al-Alam News. (Retrieved on: 13/11/2018) from: https://bit.ly/2w2lTYZ

77   "Salman Canal" built to link the Persian Gulf to the Arabian Sea at $80 Billion. 9/9/2015. Amwal Magazine. (Retrieved on: 17/10/2018) from: https://bit.ly/2w3TtNZ

a unified vision among them regarding political, security and economic strategy. This is not an easy task given that many Gulf joint ventures are still struggling to see the light."[78]

- The region is facing numerous crises, mainly in Yemen, which makes it impossible for the canal to cross the country at least before the crisis ends. In this case "the standby route crossing the Sultanate of Oman towards the Arabian Sea would be used instead."[79] This is not easy because of the tensions between Saudi Arabia and Oman, due to Muscat's close relations with Iran and its accusations by Riyadh that it smuggles weapons to the Yemeni Houthis. Therefore, Oman may refuse to cooperate with the Kingdom, "making the choice to free and stabilize Yemen a key project for Saudi Arabia to secure its borders and develop the people of both Yemen and Saudi Arabia through the new canal, leading to an unprecedented civilization renaissance in the Arab region."

- The possibility of a Saudi - UAE dispute will impact the relations between the two countries, as Abu Dhabi would be affected by this project because of its direct impact on the Jebel Ali region, which is the first regional center for logistic services in the Middle East for maritime transportation, especially after talks regarding the significant impact the Pakistani Gwadar port would have on the region. This would affect the joint strategic plans of the two countries, especially in Yemen, where there is a hidden conflict between them based on the UAE's support of the south and its desire to separate[80], in addition to its quest to control areas and islands in the mouth of the Strait of Bab-el-Mandeb.[81] Meanwhile, Saudi Arabia is impeding the UAE from establishing military

---

78 Abdul Rahman Abu Al Futuh. The "Salman Canal" what is the Saudi purpose behind this water crossing project? Op. cit. from: https://bit.ly/2KoA0uu

79 The "Salman Canal"... what is the Saudi's purpose for the project? Op. cit. from: https://bit.ly/2HJp1Kt

80 Maps: Salman competes with Suez and threatens Jebel Ali. Op. cit. from: https://bit.ly/2rdielo

81 The Emirate's invasion of Yemeni Socotra Island... the full story. 27/11/2017.

bases in Somalia[82] and Eretria[83], which it believes will impact its influence in the region.

- If a war breaks out in the GCC in the future, namely between Iran and Saudi Arabia, will Saudi Arabia be able to defend the canal against Iranian missile attacks which could cut off navigation there, if in fact, the main proposal behind this project is to avoid the Strait of Hormuz. This is also true for the Salwa Canal project (which will be tackled later). It seems that part of the arms deals made by Riyadh stem from this idea, especially the air defense weapons such as Russian S-400 and Pantsir missile systems[84] in addition to the US THAAD missile systems. In fact, these weapons are intended to be used by the KSA for protection against a potential strike from Yemen.[85]

Salwa Water Canal

The Salwa Water Canal project is also of great importance to the Kingdom, where it sees many benefits. According to many sources, it will be implemented "through a Saudi – Emirati –

Al-Arabi Al-Jadeed. (Retrieved on: 15/11/2018) from: https://bit.ly/2i6C9ll
Also see: Husein Amara. 8/5/2018. How does the Emirates justify its intervention in the strategic Yemeni island of Socotra? France 24. (Retrieved on: 17/10/2018) from: https://bit.ly/2FVFCZX

82 One of the signs of contradiction between the allies is the UAE's determination to invest in the port of Barbara in Somalia through an agreement between the company Dubai Ports and the separatist government, Somaliland. For more details, see: French patrol: Abu Dhabi is moving to invest the port of "Barbara" to achieve regional goals! 17/7/2018. Watan. (Retrieved on: 30/10/2018) from: https://bit.ly/2L4QHPB

83 Report: UAE military bases to increase influence in East Africa. 4/9/2017. Al-Jazeera. (Retrieved on: 27/10/2018) from: https://bit.ly/2exAFeE

84 Russian military resource to "RT": Lobbied by the US, the KSA abandoned S-400. 11/6/2018. Russia Today. (Retrieved on: 19/11/2018) from: https://bit.ly/2LJ2UWi
Also see: Washington threatens the KSA and Qatar with sanctions if Russian "S-400" was purchased. 14/6/2018. Russia Today. (Retrieved on: 29/10/208) from: https://bit.ly/2HOuDCs

85 Rouhani: the region's petroleum cannot be exported without the Iranian. 3/7/2018. Al-Alam News. (Retrieved on: 17/10/2018) from: https://bit.ly/2MP6kHl

Egyptian investment consortium of 9 companies in this field, initially estimated to cost 2.8 billion Saudi Riyals... The project plan is summarized as follows: A sea canal starting from the port of Salwa between Saudi Arabia and Qatar to Khawr al Udaydon the Arab - Persian Gulf, extending the eastern coast of Saudi Arabia in full and uninterrupted, considering that the border with Qatar is 60-km long." The width will be about 200m and its depth between 15m and 20m.[86]

The project is to be funded entirely by Saudi and Emirati private sector investment, with full sovereignty in Saudi Arabia, while leading Egyptian drilling companies will undertake the task of constructing the canal.[87]

Economic Utility

In this regard, economic factors can be summarized as follows:

- From available information, it appears that linking the Salman Canal with Salwa Canal at Khawr Al Udayd may make the passage of tankers to the Arab - Persian Gulf much easier.

- This canal is different from that of Salman Canal as it is in Saudi territory, which spares the country a lot of regional repercussions facing it, as previously mentioned.

- Tourism will be more active due to cruise ships which will cross the GCC countries. In addition, "regulated fishing will be promoted, reducing the temperature by at least 2 degrees Celsius, and possibly increasing rainfall in the region, minimising sandstorms and stabilizing desert soils."[88]

---

86 "Salwa" water canal... will geographic isolation be the last leverage against Qatar? 10/4/2018. Noon Post. (Retrieved on: 15/10/2018) from: https://bit.ly/2reUuxZ

87 "Salwa" water canal... will geographic isolation be the last leverage against Qatar? Op. cit. from: https://bit.ly/2reUuxZ

88 Monalisa Freiha. 7/4/2018. Salwa Canal... Does the KSA really intend to eliminate is land borders with Qatar? Annahar Lebanese Newspaper.

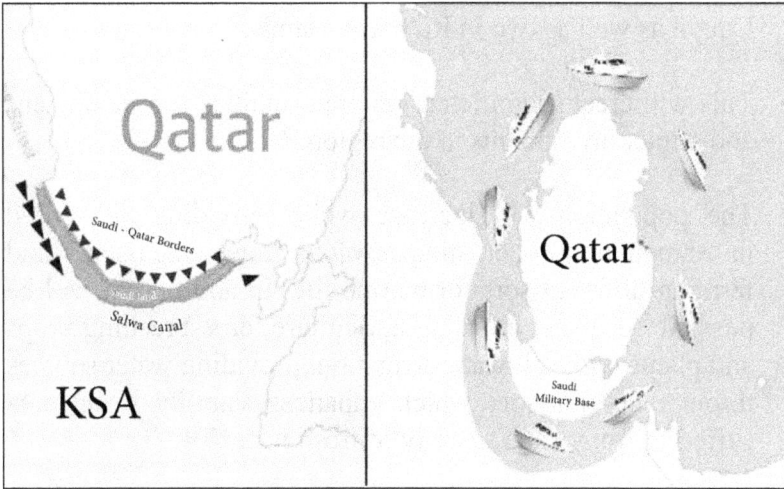

Planned Salwa Water Canal

- As for the environment, the canal "does not pass through residential villages or agricultural areas, but will revive activity in the region. The region is characterized by the quality of other scheduled projects, both oil and industrial, which qualify it to be an economic and industrial hub."[89] In addition, observers see that the reason behind selecting this region is that its sandy nature is free of obstacles impeding the implementation process, as no mountain chains or rugged terrain impede drilling operations."[90]

- Many projects to encourage tourism will be created at the canal banks. "Resorts along the new coast" are planned to be built and "constitute separate units encompassing private beaches for each resort, in addition to 5 main hotels including one in Salwa Canal, one in Al-Sikak, the third in Khawr Al

---

(Retrieved on: 27/10/2018) from: https://bit.ly/2GGBLVR
Also see: An enormous sea canal project along the Saudi - Qatari borders turning Qatar into an "island", 5/4/2018. Sabq Online Newspaper. (Retrieved on: 16/10/2018) from: https://bit.ly/2GXwGYn

89   Ibid.

90   Monalisa Freiha. Salwa Canal... Does the KSA really intend to eliminate its land borders with Qatar? Op. cit. from: https://bit.ly/2GGBLVR

Udayd as well as two in Ra's Abu Qamis."[91]

- This will create significant job opportunities for the citizens and attract investments to the region.[92]

- The population will increase while providing diversified investment options, creating new jobs, improving fishery, and farming different sorts of marine life. In addition, it will be possible to invest in saline agriculture, crossbreeding crops and plants with salt water irrigation, providing water sources through desalination, which enhances stability in an area suffering from acute scarcity of fresh water."[93]

- The area will receive ships, including "tankers and passenger ships with a total length of 295m, a maximum width of 33m and a maximum diving depth of about 12m"[94], especially if the Salman Canal project is completed in parallel.

- The KSA will be also able to collect transit tariffs from crossing carriers, providing an additional income for the treasury.

In this regard, an important factor should be noted: digging the canal will geographically isolate Qatar, separating it from Saudi Arabia, which will lead to the need to build bridges linking both countries, which will increase the indirect cost of the canal.

---

91 "Salwa" water canal... will geographic isolation be the last leverage against Qatar? Op. cit. from: https://bit.ly/2reUuxZ
Also see: Reports on a "water canal" which physically separates Qatar from the KSA. 7/4/2018. CNN Arabia. (Retrieved on: 14/11/2018) from: https://cnn.it/2JKmqjV

92 Salwa Canal... a new Saudi plan to further the siege against Qatar. 7/4/2018. Al-Jazeera. (Retrieved on: 29/10/2018) from: https://bit.ly/2KrQ5Qn

93 An enormous sea canal project along the Saudi - Qatari borders turning Qatar into an "island". Op. cit. from: https://bit.ly/2GXwGYn

94 "Salwa" water canal... will geographic isolation be the last leverage against Qatar? Op. cit. from: https://bit.ly/2reUuxZ

Security Reasons

Many analysts see many reasons for drilling the canal:

- Protecting energy security and oil access, as previously mentioned in the context of the Salman Canal, where ships can enter from the northern part of the Arab - Persian Gulf to the canal, and then head to Salman Canal reaching the Arabian Sea away from Strait of Hormuz.

- The KSA seeks to keep oil transportation routes under its sovereign control so that it avoids threats in the event of any future conflicts in the region. Information suggests that despite its low width of 200m the canal "will be fully Saudi, and no one will be entitled to any rights in it as it will remain within the Saudi territory."[95] Subsequently, it will be open to traffic according to the rules of international law.

Geo-political Justifications

Some analysts point to other purposes for this canal project, mainly:

- The existence of a political goal that isolates Qatar from its geographical environment after the escalation of the conflict between the two countries, which are mainly due to historical reasons that periodically re-emerge.[96] In addition, the border between them was the scene of violent clashes in the past, including the 1992 firearm attack in which 3 people were killed.[97]

- There is talk about the intention to establish a Saudi military

---

95   Reports on a "water canal" which physically separates Qatar from the KSA. Op. cit. from: https://cnn.it/2JKmqjV

96   Alwan N. Amin Eddine. 2015. Globalization and Sovereignty in International and Regional Relations. Op. cit. P: 135.

97   The story of Saudi Canal of Salwa which will turn the Qatar peninsula into an island. 7/4/2018. BBC Arabia. (Retrieved on: 12/10/2018) from: https://bbc.in/2JsVhCL

base in part of the land between the Qatari border and the Salwa Canal[98], significantly besieging Doha. Information suggests the reason would be to create a military area to protect and monitor the canal.[99] This will be suggested to the "relevant authorities such as the Department of Defense and border guards to identify safe zones and ideal locations for the base."[100]

- The development of Iran - Qatar relations after the Gulf crisis has caused great concern for Riyadh in terms of the development of an Achilles heel in the East, which is a justification for provoking future crises with the Kingdom. Thus, Saudi Arabia is trying to protect its borders in concerning locations, including the use of geopolitical isolation as a policy. This will secure its vital space to a certain extent especially with the existence of a hot spot in Bahrain which may affect its Eastern province.

- It has been suggested that this project is intended to "put pressure on Qatar after multiple communications and endeavors to tighten relations and eliminate disparities between the GCC countries have failed. This is a new tug-of-war game between the parties" as "no outlook for solutions exists anymore and attempts to mend fences have failed. We are now in an escalation, rather than de-escalation period of the crisis."[101]

---

98 "Salwa" water canal… will geographic isolation be the last leverage against Qatar? Op. cit. from: https://bit.ly/2reUuxZ
    Also see: An enormous sea canal project along the Saudi - Qatari borders turning Qatar into an "island". Op. cit. from: https://bit.ly/2GXwGYn

99 Monalisa Freiha. Salwa Canal… Does the KSA really intend to eliminate is land borders with Qatar? Op. cit. from: https://bit.ly/2GGBLVR

100 Reports on a "water canal" which physically separates Qatar from the KSA. Op. cit. from: https://cnn.it/2JKmqjV
    Also see An enormous sea canal project along the Saudi - Qatari borders turning Qatar into an "island". Op. cit. from: https://bit.ly/2GXwGYn

101 Ala'a Abdul Rahman. 7/4/2018. "Salwa canal"… Has Riyadh exhausted its options to lobby Qatar? Arabi 21 (Retrieved on: 17/11/2018) from: https://bit.ly/2Fw7UKp

At the same time, many analysts have noted factors that make this project unfeasible, namely the following:

- No real economic benefits will be gained in this project as the cost will highly exceed its financial returns. It doesn't have "any strategic dimension and is not worth spending a single dollar on."[102]

- With the East – West Pipeline[103], it will be easier for the KSA to preserve energy security while increasing the pipeline's pumping capacity and numbers through routes that already exist.

- Any military or warfare motivation behind the project will be a "hostile action which will lead to the segregation of peoples and geographical lands."[104]

- US Forbes magazine also pointed out that this project is illogical especially because it is based on developing touristic resorts whereas "the area is inhabited and away from any main industrial centers. Supposing that borders with Qatar remain closed, this means that one of the main markets targeting trade or touristic activities will remain continuously closed. It doesn't make sense either to move ship traffic coming from the north or the south and divert their route to a narrow water canal away from the Gulf itself."[105]

- According to many studies, Qatar will be able to evade the

102   Monalisa Freiha. Salwa Canal… Does the KSA really intend to eliminate is land borders with Qatar? Op. cit. from: https://bit.ly/2GGBLVR

103   Aqeel Anzi. 6/7/2017. Aramco increases the East - West line intake capacity to 5 million barrels a day. Al-Riyadh Newspaper. (Retrieved on: 16/11/2018) from: http://www.alriyadh.com/950275

104   Ala'a Abdul Rahman. "Salwa canal"… Has Riyadh exhausted its options to lobby Qatar? Op. cit. from: https://bit.ly/2Fw7UKp

105   "Salwa" water canal… will geographic isolation be the last leverage against Qatar? Op. cit. from: https://bit.ly/2reUuxZ
      Also see: An enormous sea canal project along the Saudi-Qatari borders turning Qatar into an "island". Op. cit. from: https://bit.ly/2GXwGYn

imposed siege, especially when trade lines are opened with Iran via sea routes in the Gulf. This happened at the onset of the crisis with Qatar in order to provide the necessary supplies back then, and preserved its economy when the goal was for it to collapse.

It is necessary now to look at the implementation aspects of such projects in terms of real economic feasibility within the framework of the Vision 2030, or political or geo-political considerations.

Conclusion

This book strove to make a comprehensive presentation of a number of issues that are currently considered important, especially those issues that may have serious repercussions on the future of humanity.

The future relies on cooperation between countries for the good of their people and their welfare. However, things are not going in a promising direction. History shows that the most major wars have taken place following economic crises and stagnation, accompanied by an arms race by the major powers. In fact, these powers today are producing new types of tactical and strategic weapons, especially those weapons capable of carrying large warheads or are able to be undetectable by radar.

Many countries are attempting to develop offensive – defensive systems as a deterrent rather than for actual use. The International Paradigm (or the so-called World Order) has not yet stabilized as the US's uni-polar system faces major crises. Meanwhile, many other countries such as China and Russia are seeking to find a balance in the system by creating a multi-polar scheme to relieve the world tensions and reduce the potential for conflict.

In conclusion, the hope is that the strategic research material in this book will contribute to enriching the debate. It is important to increase the interaction of ideas in order to find common ground for agreement and for the good of mankind.

List of References

English References

Amin Eddine, Alwan N. 2017. Sino - German Relations 1990 – 2015: In Light of Economic Strategies and Policies. Isticharia. Beirut – Lebanon. First Edition.

Belkin, Paul. 20/5/2009. German Foreign and Security Policy: Trends and Transatlantic Implications. Congressional Research Service.

Branscomb. Lewis M. No date. Safety and Security in Megacities. Harvard University.

Egelhof, J. No date. Megacity Challenges: A stakeholder perspective. Siemens.

Mega Cities. Jan 2013. EURAMET - European Association of National Metrology Institutes.

Muzalevsky, Roman. 1/10/2010. The Kazakh-Russian "Eurasia" Canal: The Geopolitics of Water, Transport, and Trade. Eurasia Daily Monitor. Vol: 7. Issue No.: 177.

Arabic References

Al-Rifai, A. Rana & Qubaisi, Dr. Mohamad. 2004. America and the New Middle East. Dar Al Haref Al-Arabi for Printing and Publishing. Beirut – Lebanon. First Edition.

Amin Eddine, Alwan N. 2015. Globalization and Sovereignty in International and Regional Relations. Dar Abaad. Beirut – Lebanon. First Edition.

Think Tanks

Al-Azhar Observatory for Combating Extremism
American Council for Kosovo
European Association of National Metrology Institutes
European Centre for Counterterrorism and Intelligence Studies - Germany & Netherlands
Global Research & Analysis
Harmoon Center For Contemporary Studies

Heinrich Böll Foundation
International Institute for Iranian Studies
International Intelligence Community - INFORMNAPALM
Sita Institute
South Front
The James Town Foundation
Washington Institute for Near East Policy

Periodical

Al-Arab Magazine
Al-Majalla
Arabic Defense Magazine
International Review of the Red Cross
Investigation Journalism
Lebanese Army Magazine
Rose al-Yūsuf Magazine

Newspapers

Al-Ahram
Al-Akhbar Lebanese
Al-Araby Al-Jadeed
Al-Bayan UAE
Al-Eqtisadiah
Al-Hayat
Al-Ittihad
Al-Jarida Iraqi
Al-Masry Al-Youm
Al-Moatamar Iraqi
Al-Quds Al-Arabai
Al-Rai Jordanian
Al-Raya Qatari
Al-Rayah Qatari
Al-Riyadh Saudi
Al-Wasat Bahrain
Al-Watan
Al-Watan Kuwaiti
Al-Youm
Annahar Lebanese
Asharq Al-Awsat

List of References

Assafir Lebanese
China People's Daily Online
Dostor Egyptian
Elbalad
Elshaab Al-Jadeed
Eurasia Daily Monitor
Le Monde
Masrawy
Rai Al-Youm
Sabq Online
Sout Al- Omma
The Daily Caller
The Daily Star
The New Khalij
Watan
Youm 7

News Channels and Sites
24.ae
Afri-gate News
Al-Aged News
Al-Alam News
Al-Arabiya
Al-Hurra
Al-Jazeera
AlKhalij Online
Al-Manar
Al-Mayadeen
Al-Monitor
Al-Sumaria
Al-Watan Voice
Al-Yawm Channel
Anadolu Agency
Arabi 21
Arabi Press
Arabian Business
Arabic China
Astute News
BBC Arabia
CNBC Arabia

CNN Arabia
Dawn
DW
Elaph
El-Marada
Elnahra
El-Watan News
Emirates News Agency (WAM)
Erem news
Fraeen News
France 24
Geiroon
Horria Post
Lebanon Debate
Misr Al Arabia
Monte Carlo International
National Kuwait
National News Agency - Lebanon
Noon Post
Reddit
Reuters
Roayah News
Rudaw Media Network
Russia Today
Sasa Post
Shaam Network
Sky News Arabia
Sputnik
TRT Arabia
Turk Press
United Nations
USA Today
Wikipedia